THE QUICK & EASY VEGETARIAN COOKBOOK

NEW, REVISED AND EXPANDED EDITION

THE QUICK & EASY VEGETARIAN COOKBOOK

RUTH ANN MANNERS & WILLIAM MANNERS

M. EVANS AND COMPANY, INC.
NEW YORK

Reiterated, though no less heartfelt, thanks to all those whose help made *The Quick & Easy Vegetarian Cookbook* a possibility. And now the same deeply felt thanks go to all our friends and relatives: the recipe developers, tasters, suggesters, the objecters-to and in-favor-ofs, et cetera, et cetera.

M. Evans and Company, Inc.
216 East 49th Street
New York, New York 10017

ISBN 1-56865-133-3

Manufactured in the United States of America

Still for Tracy, Tim,
Jane, Julie, Michael,
Jonathan, and Paul

Contents

Introduction

When a friend learned we were writing a vegetarian cookbook, she reacted by writing to us immediately: "Too bad to be so lazy, but for a noncook like me a cholesteric hamburger will always be easier to prepare—or even to eat raw—than anything needing chopping, slicing, blending, mixing."

Her statement was made fifteen years ago, when there were very few vegetarians, but it can still be regarded as a summation of *People* v. *Vegetarian Cookery*. So now, as then, we feel that our book may well perform a public service if it helps make vegetarian cuisine quick and easy. By being quick and easy, this cuisine may also help do away with the desperate need felt by many people for packaged convenience foods, with their chemicals and high prices. Confirmed vegetarians may very well profit in a special way. We hope our recipes will make it possible for them to enjoy dishes they've desired with gourmet passion but feared to tackle because of their complexity and long preparation time.

Still, we realize it's natural to be leery of shortcut cooking. It calls to mind fast-food franchises, stamped-out meals, and instant soups straight from the lab. It does not follow, however, that long preparation time is essential to excellence. (A restaurant in New York that specializes in soups had a sign proclaiming its lentil soup was four and a half hours in the making, implying that this made their soup beyond compare.) The proof of the pudding continues to be in the eating, not in the length of time required to prepare it. Testing our recipes therefore included tasting the finished products—by us and our friends and relatives.

Sound nutrition, the best sickness-prevention medicine, also entered into the creation of our recipes. We have avoided the use of refined ingredients, ingredients that are nutritionally suspect, and an abundance of eggs, cream, butter, cheese, or any ingredient that can clog arteries. We also favor fresh fruits and vegetables, whole grains, and legumes. Our soups do not consist of a canned soup camouflaged with noncanned embellishments.

We felt that our recipes should contribute not only to health, and this included minimizing the energy that the cook expended, but also to conservation of fuel, an objective to be aimed at today more than ever. There's no reason, for example, why foods cannot continue baking after the oven has been turned off. All that this change in procedure requires is some precise calculation. If a dish calls for 30 minutes of baking at 400°, the oven might be turned off after 20 minutes and the dish allowed to remain in the oven while it cools for 15 or 20 minutes. (The unobtainable fuel-conservation ideal is to put food to be baked in a cold oven and to take it out, completely done, from a cold oven.) Top-of-the-range dishes are also fuel savers, as are undercooking rather than overcooking, using a pressure cooker whenever possible, and microwaving when feasible.

Certain terms require definition. What is *quick*? What is *easy*? Obviously, if an entrée is prepared in 5 minutes, it is quick. But is it still quick if it takes three times that long? The answer is yes, when "three times that long" is still comparatively fast. For example, eggplant parmigiana usually takes a half hour to prepare; if it can be done in half that time, we think it deserves to be regarded as quick. And we shall declare an entrée quick and easy even though it requires considerable cooking or baking time after it has been quickly and easily prepared.

Easy is also determined by comparison. Recipes that eliminate preparation steps and that are simplified in every possible way are obviously easier. When a recipe is easy, you know without question that it is, just as you know when one is difficult. It should also be noted that the preparation time we've specified for a particular recipe is merely an approximation. Don't let it make you rush madly around the kitchen or feel inferior if you can't complete a recipe in the time stated.

In spite of these assurances, the book's recipes may still evoke visions of an athletic event with stopwatch in hand and records to be made. Our intention is far different; we simply want to offer a wholesome, delicious cuisine that's easily achieved.

The recipes are presented as they are for the sake of simplicity, clarity, and convenience. In many cookbooks, recipes start with a list of all the ingredients required, followed by directions for their use. To minimize the time it takes to find the ingredients referred to, we have not separated them from the directions. Instead, we have set them in boldface and put them directly ahead of the directions that apply to them. Thus, as you move along in a recipe, you will be able to tell more easily what ingredients are needed and how they are to be used.

We hope this book will be especially helpful to the following:

- Those who are always on the lookout for new meatless recipes, whether easy or difficult.
- The husband and wife who both spend the day at work and have little time for cooking.
- College students who have neither the time nor the money for complicated dishes but have a ravenous passion for food.
- Those who want to save money.
- Those who believe vegetarian cooking is too difficult or too dull.
- Those interested in health, natural food, and animal rights.
- Those who want an occasional dietary change.

The vegetarian hiker, camper, or boatowner whose cooking facilities are limited and who wants to relax while on vacation but still not subsist on canned beans or their equivalent.

Nonvegetarians who have a vegetarian child or two and have to prepare two menus.

Nonvegetarians who have vegetarian friends they would like to entertain.

And finally, we hope this book will help avid gardeners who find themselves with a bumper crop on their hands and need easy ways to use their produce.

Timesaving Approaches

Wonderful though timesaving mechanical aids may be, the human element—when understood and exploited—can help in getting things done in the kitchen. The right approach springs from a well-known command: "If you can't stand the heat, get out of the kitchen!" And there can be all kinds of heat, all kinds of pressure: The bread's not rising. Why has the cake fallen? The company will arrive any minute now, and I'm not dressed and I have the salad to do and the kitchen looks like a disaster area and . . . and . . . and. . . .

There *are* answers.

1. Ignore the rationalization that you save time by not keeping an orderly kitchen as you go along. Ignore it because it's false. A disorderly kitchen causes you to waste time. It trips you up physically and makes you wretched mentally. We know a role model for all nonprofessionals, a short-order cook who, besieged by what seems an impossible number of orders, manages to remain unflustered. All his motions are smooth, quick, and effortless; and they include wiping the counter whenever it needs it, putting dishes away, and keeping pots and pans in their places.

2. Be sure you have all the ingredients you need for a recipe before you start. For example, it's frustrating and a waste of time to start making a pasta dish, only to discover that you're out of the sauce you need.

3. When a dinner party looms, you'll be serene if you've planned and prepared ahead, lightening the burden by doing a little over several days instead of trying to do everything at once.

4. Know a recipe thoroughly before you start. Just reading it over a few times isn't enough, for you'll still have to refer to it again and again. Time will actually be saved if you memorize the recipe. This will also give you the feeling of power that a creator enjoys; creators, after all, don't have to refer to the work of others.

5. We have found that it's possible to do a recipe much more quickly and easily by making it a number of successive times. Familiarity, in this instance, breeds assurance. But you may meet with a degree of hostility from those who find themselves, in their words, "always eating the same old thing." To avoid this emotional situation, simply alter the oft-repeated recipe just a bit. For example, the appearance and flavor of the dessert you've been making regularly can be

changed merely by using a different sweetener and/or a different kind of nut or fruit.

6. Memorize basic measurements. This will make it unnecessary for you to look them up each and every time-wasting time. For example, it's helpful to know that there are 3 teaspoons in 1 tablespoon. When a recipe calls for 4 teaspoons, you'll be able to take care of that with 1 tablespoon and 1 teaspoon instead of laboriously measuring out 4 individual teaspoons. Or if you can't find your ¼-cup measure, or it needs washing, it's handy to know that 4 tablespoons equal ¼ cup.

7. Always have the tools you need readily available. Measuring spoons have the habit of straying, so it's a good idea to have so many that you never need to look for one. Have an abundance of measuring cups, too. Though they can't hide themselves as readily as measuring spoons, they're so often dirty just when needed that it seems eerily more than coincidence.

Essential kitchen aids should always be of the best and in good shape: for example, knives sharp, the measurements on glass measuring cups not eroded to unreadability.

The accessibility of items in the refrigerator is also vital. This is made possible by your orderly mind—orderly in the kitchen if not elsewhere. It always sees to it that a particular item is invariably on the same shelf and at the same spot on that shelf. This eliminates a great deal of time spent in frantic search. It also helps to store food in transparent containers, so that you don't find yourself struggling with the tight-fitting lid of an opaque container only to discover it doesn't hold what you want.

8. Another dictum for the orderly mind: To avoid the time-consuming quandary of not remembering whether you've put a certain ingredient in the mixing bowl, always use ingredients in the order in which they're presented in a recipe.

9. Remember—as brutal experience has taught—that you can only do a limited amount in a brief period. Plan a meal accordingly. Even when using quick and easy recipes, it's an error to attempt to prepare seven courses in a half hour. That's strictly for fantasy.

Timesaving Equipment

Finely chopped, thinly sliced, grated, ground, and *minced* are key words in vegetarian recipes. They are also probably the reason why vegetarian cooking has a reputation for taking too much time, too much work, and too much bother.

Is the reputation deserved? Certainly.

Is the reputation necessary? Absolutely not!

There are huge, gaping loopholes through which you can avoid all the drudgery and dog work in vegetarian cooking!

But, first, why all the slicing, chopping, and grating? There are good reasons for it. Orientals have known for centuries that reducing food to small bits before cooking: enhances the flavor by blending textures; increases eye appeal by preserving bright, fresh colors; and saves fuel cost by greatly shortening cooking time. Perhaps all these benefits were more important to them than saving time and work.

What the Chinese and Japanese may not have realized, as they quickly tossed and cooked their food by the stir-fry method, was that they were also preserving its nutritive value.

Today, thousands of years later, we still want to enjoy all these benefits and also save time and work. And we can.

So now for the loopholes! Simply put, they are the excellent mechanical devices that do all your chopping, slicing, and grating for you—and a few other things besides.

Obviously, much of the chopping and cutting can be done with a set of good-quality, sharp, heavy knives. With considerable practice, you may even become as adept as a hibachi chef. But if time is money and the kitchen is not the place to spend it, then consider the helpers we describe here.

We are not suggesting that you must have them all (you'd probably soon run out of storage space or money or both), but these tools and equipment win our vote. Some of them may seem expensive, but one small machine can often take the place of a whole kitchen clutter of small gadgets and, in the end, cost no more.

Heavy-Duty Food Preparer

Most people call it a *mixer*, but it's much more than that. It can be the genie of your kitchen if you get one that has the sinew and muscle to do everything you command. Certainly, it must be big, heavy, powerful, and versatile.

Our own personal genie is a KitchenAid. Ours is a home version of a commercially used machine. The mass-produced, competitively priced mixers that most people buy just don't compare. It is expensive; but you'll get so much more use and pleasure out of it, you won't regret its price. If you buy a lighter-duty model, you may be sorry. You just won't be able to use it for as many things or as often.

The paraprofessional heavy-duty machine we're talking about does everything. It has a flat beater for cakes, pastry, mashed potatoes, et cetera. It has a wire whip for eggs, mayonnaise, milk drinks, and so on. It has a dough hook for kneading yeast breads.

With attachments, it's also a juice extractor, colander and sieve, food grinder, slicer and shredder, ice-cream freezer, can opener, and even grain mill. The grain mill attachment is a special gem. By making it possible to grind whole grains as needed, it eliminates the necessity to refrigerate whole-grain flours to prevent their becoming rancid. You can buy whole grains in quantity and grind them as the occasion arises. You can also create your own special combinations and blends.

The KitchenAid is a rather large machine that may cause space problems in a tiny kitchen. Ideally, it should be kept at the ready on the counter, with its attachments in a drawer nearby, so that you can call upon it without ado. If you have to drag it out of storage each time it's used, you may be disinclined to make the most of this beautiful, valuable genie.

Food Processor

This little miracle worker originated in France as a large, commercial-sized processor designed for restaurant use. Then someone had the bright idea of making a smaller version for the home kitchen, and the Cuisinart food processor was born. This small machine is rarely seen in French home kitchens, but when it was imported to this country, it caught on immediately and revolutionized food preparation from Maine to California.

What can it do for you? It can slice, grate, mince, shred, and purée the daylights out of any kind of food you might care to feed it. All those tedious jobs that used to slow you down can be performed in seconds.

In addition, the food processor can produce a flaky piecrust, make smooth nut butters, blend salad dressings, turn frozen fruit into instant sherbet, make dry cottage cheese into a low-calorie cream cheese substitute, and much more.

Naturally, the great success of the Cuisinart has spawned a flood of imitations. Most of them are less expensive, but not all of them are as good as the original. If you buy a food processor, you'll probably soon wonder how you got along without it.

Blender

The blender has been around for a long time. When Waring first introduced it, it created much the same kind of excitement as the Cuisinart food processor. It's a great little machine and can do many of the things that a food processor does, but on a smaller scale. Instead of doing a batch in a single operation, you may have to divide ingredients into small portions and complete the processing in several loads. Besides being slower than a processor, the blender's results, in some cases, are of somewhat lesser quality. There are some processing tasks it simply cannot handle.

Food processor owners, however, are not likely to discard their blenders. There are some things a blender can do better than a food processor, such as beating air into a milk shake, smoothie, or Marguerita. It's better for liquifying tomatoes, peaches, and bananas. This has something to do with the size and shape of the two containers. It's also better for doing small quantities, and more convenient to store in the refrigerator and pour from when making crepes. Blender and processor can be used in tandem, doing part of a recipe in one and part in the other. You can even make it a ménage à trois and bring the KitchenAid food preparer into the act. This combination certainly speeds things up.

Blenders take little space, are easily moved from one place to another, and are not outrageously expensive. They are a special boon to the student living in a dormitory and to the apartment dweller with a minuscule kitchen.

In buying a blender, you'll be wise to invest in one of the better models from a well-known manufacturer. You may find that it has fewer push buttons and gadgetry. After all, who needs such an infinite variety of speeds? Models with no more than eight push buttons, with their larger size and more convenient spacing, are easier to use and clean.

Microwave

Let us sing the praises due the microwave: its versatility and its fast-cooking and nutrient-saving abilities.

It's a shame that some people use their microwaves merely to defrost or reheat foods. It's capable of doing so much more. It can bring your cup of water for tea to a boil in perhaps 2 minutes. (It's so fast because it heats the inside and the outside at the same time.) In 5 seconds, it makes a clove of garlic easier to peel. At reduced power, it can be used to keep food warm. When the kids come home from school, they can easily and safely reheat the food you've left for them.

Aside from its speed, of all cooking techniques it saves the most nutrients, and needs little water or none at all. The microwave is an energy saver. It doesn't add heat to a kitchen on a hot day, and it reduces cleanup time considerably. Should we go on singing its praises? We could easily.

You don't have to buy new cookware to use in a microwave. While you can't use metal pots, any ovenproof glass and most ceramics and porcelains (except those decorated with gold or other metals) are perfect. The instruction book that accompanies any microwave gives all the details.

Note:
The microwave used in testing the recipes in this book is 700 to 900 watts. If your microwave has a different wattage, adjust cooking times accordingly.

Additional Helpers and Timesavers

Pressure Cooker

We feel that your cooking will be quicker and easier if you have a pressure cooker, either aluminum or stainless steel. It does a superbly swift job of cooking vegetables and legumes. As our recipes will show, it's also marvelous for preparing soups and vegetable stews.

There are a couple of drawbacks, however. Since you can't see what's going on in a pressure cooker and can't easily lift the lid to check, it's easy to overcook foods. Therefore, follow recommended times carefully. The other drawback is the fear some people have of pressure cookers. They do hiss occasionally, but the hiss is no more harmful than a pussycat's and doesn't predict dire things.

The 6-quart pressure cooker, we feel, is a more useful size than the 4-quart version. No matter what the size, the stainless steel cooker has virtues lacking in aluminum cookers. It's easier to clean and there's no possibly hazardous aluminum to be absorbed by the cooking foods.

Juice Extractor

When Emerson asked his good friend Thoreau what dish he preferred, he said, "The nearest." His simplify-simplify philosophy had provided that answer. And he surely would have looked disapprovingly at a juice extractor.

Helen and Scott Nearing, the masters of the good and simple life, had an extractor but felt somewhat guilty about it. They confessed, however, that they could not resist their "weekly ambrosia," a mix of carrot, apple, and beet juice.

Such ambrosias are now viewed as nutritional supplements. Moreover, juice recipes provide you with blends aimed at handling common ailments.

No matter what the blend, the drinks are delicious. The only reason for not drinking them oftener is the chore of cleaning the extractor after each use. We've found the Juiceman II takes care of that by uniting its blade and juice strainer. It's quiet, too. There are also no vibrations because the vegetable or fruit pulp goes into a separate container and therefore doesn't throw the machine off balance.

Freshly extracted juices can be used as ingredients in soups and dips or added to main dishes and salad dressings for extra nutrients and flavor. The pulp, a good source of fiber, should be saved and added to sauces (a healthful thickener), main dishes, baked goods, and toppings. Or throw the pulp on the compost heap, where it will add to the heap's other organic matter.

Finally, juice extractors are a quick and easy way to get vitamins and minerals that your regular diet may not be providing.

Electric Knife

What we like best about our electric knife is the way it slices bread. Even bread that's oven-fresh can be neatly sliced to any thickness; and loaves with thick, crisp crusts don't end up mangled and squashed. The electric knife can also be used to slice cheeses, vegetables, and frozen foods.

Collapsible Vegetable Steamer

This handy little basket is made of stainless steel and can adjust to fit nearly any pan. It stands on three legs to keep the food to be steamed out of the water and has a small lifting handle in the center.

Knives

Years ago, a dispute raged: The clean, stainless-steel knife advocates battled those who favored the carbon-steel knife in spite of its rusting and staining qualities. That was years ago. Now you can buy stain-free, high-carbon-steel knives with plastic handles, which make them dishwasher safe. That, we believe, is the one to buy. We like Henckels.

But ease of cleaning is perhaps less important in a knife than sharpness and its ability to keep a keen edge. A sharp knife does an easier, faster, better job than a dull one. And if you're afraid that you may cut yourself handling sharp knives, remember you may be cut as readily by a dull knife.

Metal Pans

Metal pans have the advantages of light weight and not breaking. But all pans cannot be praised. Beware of cheap ones; they're usually too thin. If you use them, your food ends up burnt on the outside and underdone on the inside. What you should be looking for are pans that are made of heavy tinned steel. You'll make no mistake in getting the kind professionals use. They're easy to clean; and because they have a thick nonstick coating, they're scratch resistant. And since they last a long time, they're a better buy than those whose cheap price may have attracted you in the first place.

Nonstick Pots and Pans

All nonstick pans are not alike. This time, at least, the old bromide that "you get what you pay for" is true. Avoid nonstick pans offered as a special of three pans in a package. It's not just that their life is short; their performance during their brief life is inferior:

1. They require using more oil or butter when sautéing. Good pans will perform with almost no fat.

2. Their cleanup is more difficult. Good pans come clean with just a swipe.

The non-sale pans are better designed and manufactured. The nonstick coating is heavier and includes the rim edge. Sides may come down at an efficient angle to allow more cooking surface. Their heft is better, which means better heat conductivity. Their bottoms are heavier and won't bow the way thinner bottoms do; they will remain flat.

To top it off, they're cheaper. Though the initial price may be three or four times that of the cheapies, they'll last five to ten times as long.

Slicers, Graters, and Choppers

If you haven't been blessed with power slicing and grating equipment, you should consider several manual devices that can do an excellent job of cutting food into small bits.

We've found the four-sided, stainless steel grater–slicer that sits squarely on the counter and that one holds steady by a handle at the top to be more satisfactory and safer than the single-sided type that must be held at an angle or laid flat across the bowl.

The mandoline is a first-rate slicing tool. It rests at an angle on the counter and can be adjusted to vary the thickness of slices.

Mouli graters, imported from France, may appear inconsequential, but they do have virtues. For one thing, they're very handy for grating small amounts of cheese or nuts. Another very real convenience is that you can grate directly into the cooking pot or over the top of a casserole.

One of our favorite gadgets is a tiny nutmeg grater, which we hang on a hook so that it is in clear view. It has a small compartment that holds one nutmeg ready to be grated. No need to get out the nutmeg jar and round up a grater. It's all right there!

The chef's knife should also be your knife for general chopping and mincing. It comes in different lengths and has a triangular blade. All you do is put its point on the chopping block; then, with a downward, rhythmic movement, do your chopping and mincing. All it takes is a little practice—very little, really.

Two-handled rocker knives are excellent for chopping mushrooms and herbs. Perhaps you'd prefer the professional model, which has three blades.

Other Helpful Tools

And here is a list (in alphabetical order) of other small helpers that we feel should be in the well-equipped kitchen:

Biscuit cutter

Coffee grinder (good, too, for grinding agar flakes to powder and for chopping fresh herbs and toasted whole spices)

Colander

Cookbook holder (transparent plastic)

Egg-white separator

Electric skillet

Food mill

Garlic press

Grapefruit knife

Kitchen shears

Melon baller

Pastry brush

Pastry cloth and knit rolling pin cover

Small electric chopper/grinder (good for grinding coffee, chopping vegetables, mincing garlic, and much more)

Spatulas (several—flexible plastic is better than rubber. It's dishwasher safe and doesn't get gummy. You may want one or more metal spatulas, as well as hard non-metal ones for non-stick cookware)

Spinning salad dryer

Strainer

Swivel potato peeler

Thermometers (yeast, candy)

Timer

Tongs

Vegetable brush

Wire whisks (several sizes)

Wooden spoons (large ones for mixing)

Procedures and Ingredients

Many entrées could be quickly prepared if it were not for an ingredient that requires considerable cooking time. For example, if you have cooked beans on hand, you can swiftly complete many recipes you might otherwise have to rule out.

Many other ingredients and recipe elements can be prepared ahead and in quantity, so that when a recipe specifies them, no precious time is lost. The list includes piecrusts, crepes, brown rice, curry sauce, spaghetti sauce, grated cheese, chopped nuts, bread crumbs, and all the legumes. Many of these foods can be kept in the refrigerator for a week or longer. Some can be stored in the freezer for several months.

If you do a thorough job of building this kind of a stockpile, some meals may be more a matter of assembling ingredients than of cooking. And often, this is a most welcome situation.

Bread freezes beautifully. If sliced before freezing, only the amount needed can be removed without thawing the whole loaf. If you are freezing an unsliced loaf, cool it on a rack after baking and place it unwrapped in the freezer. When frozen, seal it in an airtight plastic bag.

Bread crumbs made from your own homemade bread are more flavorful than the packaged kind you buy at the store. They will keep for a long time in jars in the refrigerator or can be stored in the freezer. Get into the habit of tossing all the end pieces and bits of bread that have become too dry for other use into the blender or food processor for crumbs. And if you want bread crumbs better than those made from plain bread, use English muffins.

Small bread rounds are useful to have on hand for canapé bases. Occasionally, when baking bread, save some of the dough and bake it in little tomato paste cans. The tiny loaves bake quickly and can be sliced into thin rounds, toasted, spread on a tray to freeze, then packaged in plastic bags.

Broth cubes and powders. The good news is that there are many vegetable broth products on the market. But read the labels. Many contain no preservatives or dubious chemicals. Even major manufacturers like Knorr, whose products are available worldwide, have brought out "Vegetarian Vegetable Bouillon." One of their cubes, containing hydrolized protein, onions, carrots, leeks, cabbage, parsley, and garlic, makes 2 cups of broth. It also contains monosodium glutamate (MSG) and salt which you may find objectionable. But there is no MSG in dehydrated onion soup mix by Lipton, McCormick, and Campbell's. What they do have are "natural flavors." Masquerading under that term are animal-derived (beef, poultry, or fish) products. So just reading the label may be deceptive.

Among better broth powders are those made by the SOUPerior Bean & Spice Company of Clackamas, Oregon, and available by mail from Harvest Direct (1-800-835-2867). Their broths come in three flavors—vegetable, chicken, and beef—none of which contains animal products, chemicals, or preservatives. Two teaspoons of the powder make a cup of broth. The chicken and beef flavors are designed primarily for "transitional vegetarians." Your natural food market may carry a French onion soup mix by Mayacamas that lists neither MSG nor "natural flavors" among its ingredients. Incidentally, the law does not require the listing of MSG.

Cheese. Whenever possible, use only freshly grated cheese. However, for emergencies have bags or jars of grated cheese in the refrigerator or freezer to pour out and use. It's a good way to use all the little ends and bits of leftover cheese that might otherwise be wasted. Most hard cheeses freeze well, but soft cheese does not. You can keep uncreamed cottage cheese in the freezer for three or four months. Uncreamed cottage cheese can be blended until smooth in the food processor to make an excellent low-calorie, low-cost substitute for cream cheese.

Couscous is a traditional North African dish made with tiny pellets of grain prepared in a process similar to that of making pasta. Unlike rice, it cooks in as little as 3 minutes. It comes in both plain and whole wheat varieties, regular and quick-cooking. We recommend the quick-cooking, whole wheat variety. You can use it like rice—as a side dish, with vegetables, or with sauce. Add raisins, serve it with cut-up fruit, yogurt, or chopped nuts. One cup of couscous makes 2½ cups when cooked.

Dried legumes. Soybeans, chickpeas (garbanzos), navy beans, lentils, split peas, etcetera, are a valuable source of protein in any diet. They can, however, take a long time to cook, with the exception of lentils, black-eyed peas, and split peas, which do not require soaking. To prepare the other legumes for cooking, soak overnight or use the quick-soak method.

Quick-soak method: Pick over the beans and wash them. Bring water to a boil (allow about 6 cups of water for 2 cups of beans). Add the beans; and when the water again comes to a boil, cook for 2 minutes. Remove from the heat, cover the pan, and allow to stand for 1 hour. The beans are then ready for cooking.

There are several factors that affect the cooking time of dried legumes: the type of bean, its age, hardness of water, and altitude. If beans have been stored too long or at too high a temperature, they become harder and take longer to cook.

To pressure-cook beans, the easiest and fastest way to cook them, place them in the cooker and then add enough water to cover. Bring pressure to High and let beans cook until tender—for example, 12 minutes for soybeans, 6 for chickpeas. (These times are approximations.) To bring pressure down, run cold tap water on lid of cooker.

One cup of dried beans will yield $2^1/2$ to $2^3/4$ cups when cooked. Dried lentils and split peas will approximately double their volume.

If you don't choose to cook beans, you'll find many varieties available canned or frozen. Canned beans should always be drained and rinsed well—to reduce salt and other unwanted ingredients—before use.

Duxelles. These are finely minced mushrooms that have been drained of their liquid and sautéed until they are dry and brown. The result is actually the essence of mushroom flavor and can be used in countless ways: in sauces, stuffings, with vegetables, in soups, or just spread on crackers or toast as an appetizer. They will keep tightly covered in the refrigerator for several weeks, or they can be frozen. One-half pound of mushrooms will make about 1 cup of duxelles. Freeze them in small amounts; a little goes a long way. A recipe for making Duxelles can be found on page 50.

Nutritional yeast should have been called something more appetizing. However, we think that if people know what it provides in the way of nourishment, nothing will stop them from consuming it.

We use *Saccharomyces cerevisiae*, a yeast grown in molasses. Its protein is complete. It's yellow or gold in color, comes in flakes or powder, and has a good cheesy taste.

Nutritional yeast can be used in many ways. Add it to soups, sauces, or vegetables to boost nutritional value. A friend loves it on popcorn. If you want to cut down on cheese, it can be used on pizzas and on macaroni dishes. We give it a four-star recommendation.

Nuts are used extensively in vegetarian cuisine and can be very expensive if bought in small quantities. Save money by finding a store that sells them in bulk. They keep perfectly when stored in plastic bags in the freezer. Chop some in the food processor or blender so they will be ready to use in recipes that call for them. Store in small amounts in tightly closed glass jars in the refrigerator.

Olive oil and canola oil. We often specify extra-virgin olive oil in our recipes because we like the flavor it imparts. But that is exactly what some people don't want. For those who prefer a less intense olive taste, there are "light," "extra light," or "mild" extra-virgin oils. There is also available a blend of extra-virgin and canola oils. These oils have very little flavor and are light in color. Both types are monounsaturated, which means that they have been shown to be effective in lowering blood cholesterol. Extra-virgin oils are from the first pressing, are low in acid, and have been refined without the use of heat and solvents.

There are many brands of extra-virgin olive oil on the market, and they vary in taste, color and price. Experiment to find your favorite. The most expensive may not be the one you enjoy the most.

All these virtues of extra-virgin olive oils have led some people to believe that they can use as much as they like and the results will be beneficial to their health. Not so! All oil is fat and caloric and we should keep our consumption of it within reasonable limits.

Canola oil has less saturated fat than safflower or sunflower oil. The main reason for using it instead of olive oil is that it has practically no flavor, which could be a plus for those who dislike a pronounced olive taste or feel that it might compete with the other seasonings in a delicate dish. It is also much less expensive.

Pesto, made with fresh basil leaves, is one of the most delicious of all the Italian pasta sauces. It can also be used as a flavoring in salad dressings, with vegetables, in soups, as a spread on garlic French bread, et cetera.

To make 1 cup of pesto base, wash about 3 cups of basil leaves and dry on paper towels. In a food processor, blend them with 1/2 cup high-quality olive oil, 1/4 cup pine nuts or walnuts, and a pinch of salt until a smooth paste is formed. Pour mixture into an ice cube tray and freeze. When cubes are frozen, put them in a plastic bag, and store them in the freezer. (Alternately, freeze sauce flat in plastic bags with zipper-type closure. Break off pieces as needed.) The best way to thaw frozen pesto cubes is to place them in the refrigerator, tightly covered with plastic wrap the night before use. We find that adding the traditional minced garlic and Parmesan cheese at serving time results in a fresher-tasting sauce. If you wish to use less oil, substitute vegetable broth for part of it. See recipe for Pesto, Pasta, and Potatoes (page 170).

Phyllo, sometimes called *fillo, filo,* or *filla,* and also known as *strudel leaves* (the Greeks do not believe in standardization), is a dough made of flour, water, and salt and rolled into fragile, tissue-thin leaves. It is a useful ready-made pastry that can be quickly fashioned into ethereally beautiful dishes that are as delightful to eat as they are to look at.

Precooked vegetables. Most vegetables are at their peak when freshly cooked. Keeping them warm for any extended period will overcook them, and that means losing precious nutrients, as well as fresh color, texture, and flavor. Many times, however, especially when entertaining, it's inconvenient to cook vegetables at the very last minute.

The answer? Cook them in advance—and still have them at their peak. Here's how: Steam the vegetables in a collapsible steamer basket until barely crisp-tender. Do not overcook. Then immediately plunge them into a large pot of iced or very cold water. Use a lot of water so it doesn't warm up. The point is to stop the cooking almost instantly; lock in nutrients, color, and flavor; and keep the texture firm. Drain and refrigerate immediately. When ready to serve, combine seasonings and vegetables in a heavy pan and toss until throughly heated.

Vegetables prepared in this way will taste and look as if just cooked. The reason is that they are not overcooked; they're at their freshest, most flavorful best! And the water used for steaming may be saved for your vegetable stockpot.

Rice. Cooked rice can be a great time-saver, especially if you use the more nutritious brown rice that takes nearly an hour to prepare. Whenever you are cooking rice, consider doubling the amount so you will have some left over for use in a different recipe. You can keep cooked rice in the refrigerator for several days. Cold rice salad is delicious. Cooked brown rice makes a quick and tasty thickener for soups when whirled in the blender. Soaking brown rice overnight will cut the cooking time to about 20 minutes. To reheat rice, add 2 tablespoons of water for every cup of rice, stir well, and microwave for 2 minutes on High or put in the top of a double boiler or in a collapsible steamer basket set over boiling water, cover, and heat about 5 minutes, or until it is warmed through.

Sautéed mushrooms. Mushrooms come in many wonderful varieties such as oyster, cepes, straw, Portobello, cremini, shiitake, and morels, as well as the inexpensive common commercial kind. Each has its own character and flavor. Explore them all. Our favorite is shiitake with its strong, woodsy assertiveness. All are perishable, and it is sometimes difficult to use them quickly enough. If a recipe calls for less than the amount you have on hand, it's a good idea to sautée them all while you are about it, saving what's left over in a covered jar in the refrigerator for use a few days later or stashing them away in the freezer.

The best way to wash mushrooms is to drop them into a large pan of cold water and shake them around with your hands to loosen any particles of dirt. Do this quickly so that the mushrooms do not absorb water. Drain them well and dry them on a clean kitchen towel or paper towels. After cleaning and trimming the ends, mushrooms can be sautéed whole, sliced, or chopped. They must be dry at the time of cooking or they will not brown well.

When you cook mushrooms, they should not be crowded in the pan, and the small amount of oil or butter should be very hot. If you are doing a large amount or your pan is small, divide the mushrooms into several batches. To sauté ¹/₂ pound of mushrooms, heat 1 tablespoon of oil over high heat in a large, heavy skillet. Then add the mushrooms. Toss them with a spoon until well coated with oil or butter and continue tossing or shaking the pan for about 5 minutes. As soon as mushrooms are lightly browned, remove them from the heat. You may wish to reduce the heat in the last minutes. Adding a tablespoon or more of reduced-sodium soy sauce imparts a pleasing flavor.

Shiitake mushrooms. This popular variety has a more intense and woodsy flavor than common white mushrooms. It is available both fresh and dry. Dry shiitakes may be rehydrated by soaking the caps in hot water for 20 to 30 minutes or by microwaving in a covered container in a fraction of that time; follow instructions for your oven.

Slow-cooked onions. Hundreds of recipes call for sautéed onions—whether sliced, chopped, or minced. Onions of whatever variety have the best flavor when they are cooked so slowly that they do not brown but turn a beautiful golden color, and are sweet, mellow, and tender. Cook in a nonstick pan with a minimum of canola or vegetable oil for ¹/₂ hour or longer on very low heat, stirring occasionally. You may not always have the time or inclination to give them this special treatment, but if you get into the habit of sautéing more than you need (and preserving the extras), you'll find that they are a marvelous ingredient to have handy. They keep in the refrigerator for several days in a tightly covered jar or frozen in small amounts for 3 months or longer.

Tomato sauce base. When icicles are dangling from the eaves and snow is piling up along the fence, it is delightful to bring back the glorious days of summer with the taste of fresh, vine-ripened tomatoes. Tomatoes cannot be frozen successfully for use in salads or for slicing, but they can be peeled, chopped, and frozen for use in sauces, casseroles, and soups. No canned tomato product equals their taste. If you have a supply of ripe, unblemished tomatoes, on their bottom make a small x-shaped cut in their skin, drop them a few at a time into boiling water. After a minute or two, plunge them into cold water, slip off their skins, and chop by hand or in a food processor. Mix in a little lemon juice (juice of 1 lemon for 10 pounds of tomatoes) and freeze. Or make your favorite recipe for a cooked tomato sauce and freeze it. The sauce, of course, will be more of a time-saver later. Omit garlic and spices because freezing tends to alter their flavor, but you can include some fresh chopped herbs. The garlic and spices can be added when heating the frozen sauce for use in a recipe.

Textured vegetable protein. This meat analog, derived from soybeans, comes in quick-cooking granules, flakes, chunks, and strips in flavored or unflavored varieties. It is commonly referred to as TVP©, the copyright trademark of the Archer Daniels Midland Company, a primary maker of the product. TVP© is available at natural food stores, or you can order it unflavored or in such flavored varieties as curry, Italian, herbs and spice, chile, taco, and sloppy joe. The toll-free number to call for ordering or information is 1-800-8-FLAVOR. TVP© can add protein, fiber, and texture to recipes that are short of these qualities. It is low in fat, sodium, and calories and has no cholesterol. Granular TVP© may be rehydrated by soaking it in an equivalent amount of boiling water or broth for 5 to 10 minutes. Chunks and slices take longer.

Appetizers and Snacks

Most people enjoy eating with their hands. It probably harks back to the ancient communal pot, and it offers a basic pleasure, like watching an open fire, dining outdoors, sitting on the floor, or going barefoot. Part of the appeal of appetizers and snacks may well be that many of them are finger foods.

Appetizers, as a prelude to a meal, are meant to sharpen the appetite, not destroy it. For that reason, they should be quite simple and not too numerous. But they may also be served as a first course or even as the main event, and then they can be more substantial. There are occasions when it is fun to make a whole meal from a variety of savory tidbits. Serve a selection of fillings and a basket of warm pita bread, arranged for guests to help themselves and invent their own original combinations, and you can create a delightfully entertaining event as well as provide a nourishing meal.

Snacks for the after-game or after-theater crowd, the backpacking hiker, the children home from school, or the person who just doesn't feel like having a full meal can be nutritious as well as satisfy hunger.

FRUIT AND CHEESE

The simplest appetizers are often the most welcome. This one is as simple as it sounds: crisp, cold fruit slices presented with thin slices of sharp or mild cheese. If you want to introduce an additional taste sensation, add a bowl of Chura (see page 59) or Flavored Nuts and Seeds (see page 58).

PREPARATION TIME 10 MINUTES   **4 SERVINGS**

- 4   large, cold apples (firm, tart, eating variety), or 4 firm, ripe Bartlett pears
- $1/2$ pound low-fat cheese, thinly sliced
        Fresh lemon juice

Wash and core apples or pears. Cut into $1/2$-inch slices. Dip slices in lemon juice and arrange on a platter, alternating and overlapping with slices of cheese. Serve.

Note: To be really relaxed about this, simply offer a bowl of apples or pears, or a combination of the two, and let your guests add the cheese to the fruit slices as they cut them. Bunches of white grapes and a pot of brandy-flavored or wine-flavored cheese, with a spreading knife, are good additions to the scene.

RAW VEGETABLE PLATTER

An assortment of raw vegetables, along with a dip or spread, has become a popular party appetizer with a special appeal for dieters. When carefully arranged, the raw vegetable platter can be a delight to the eye. Use only the freshest of vegetables, young and crisp; clean them well; and for greatest enjoyment, serve them on a bed of crushed ice. Here are some vegetables that are especially good, with a few suggestions for preparing them.

Belgian Endive: Slice in half lengthwise and separate into individual leaves. These are a natural for scooping up dips or for stuffing with your favorite dip or spread.

Carrots: Peel and cut into sticks, or leave whole and cut gashes part of the way through along the length. Break off sections to eat.

Cauliflower: Break off flowerets and either serve whole or slice them thinly from top to bottom. To crisp, soak in ice water about 10 minutes. Drain and keep covered in refrigerator until used.

Celery: Cut into strips or chunks. Soak in ice water, drain, and chill.

Cherry Tomatoes: If stem ends are fresh and green, leave them on; otherwise, remove. For a different taste, try dipping them in light oil and rolling them in chopped fresh basil or dill.

Cucumbers: Use young ones with not too many seeds. Peel if waxed (most that you buy in the store are) and, using a fork, score lengthwise all the way around the cucumber. Then slice in 1/2-inch pieces.

Fennel: Remove leafy portions and reserve for use in salads. Separate stalks and cut into slices.

Green, Red, and/or Yellow Peppers: Cut in half, and remove all seeds and the white membrane. Cut in sections lengthwise.

Kohlrabi: Peel and cut into sticks.

Mushrooms: Leave small white mushrooms whole. If using larger mushrooms, cut sections through the cap vertically, just to the stem. Break apart sections to eat.

Radishes: Cut off the root ends but leave on a bit of the stem and a few tiny leaves if they are fresh and green.

Romaine: The very center leaves of romaine (or iceberg lettuce) make wonderful scoops for dips.

Scallions: Cut off ends and remove outer skin. Trim neatly.

Zucchini: Use very young, fresh squash. Cut off ends and cut crosswise into small sections. Or cut part of the way through, preserving the shape intact, and break into sections for eating.

CELERY FILLED WITH WATERCRESS AND TOFU

A good low-calorie appetizer. The watercress gives the creamy tofu filling a wonderful bite.

PREPARATION TIME 15 MINUTES   **MAKES 30 TO 40 CELERY PIECES**

- 1   clove garlic
- 1/4 teaspoon salt
- 1/2 sweet onion

With the blender or food processor running, drop in garlic and onion. Add salt.

- 1/2 bunch watercress (or more to taste)
- 1   pound tofu
- 1   tablespoon fresh lemon juice

Add watercress, tofu, and lemon juice and blend well.

8 to 10 celery stalks, washed and trimmed

Cut each celery stalk into 2-inch pieces and fill with tofu-watercress mixture.

CHEESE STICKS

Children will love to help you make these bread sticks, and they will also love to eat them.

PREPARATION TIME 15 MINUTES   MAKES ABOUT 18 STICKS
BAKING TIME 8 TO 10 MINUTES
Preheat oven to 475°.

- $3/4$ cup whole wheat flour
- $1/4$ cup unbleached all-purpose flour
- $1/4$ teaspoon dry mustard
- 3   tablespoons unsalted butter

Sift the dry ingredients together and cut in butter.

- 1   teaspoon nutritional yeast
- $1/2$ cup shredded low-fat Cheddar cheese
- $1/2$ cup freshly grated Parmesan cheese

Mix in yeast and cheeses.

- 1   egg white
- $1/8$ cup canola oil
- 3 to 4 drops of water
- Poppy or sesame seeds (optional)

Mix in egg white, oil, and the least amount of water to form a smooth dough. By hand, roll small pieces of dough into thin bread sticks about 6 inches long. Sprinkle with poppy or sesame seeds or a combination of the two if you like. Place the sticks on an oil-sprayed cookie sheet so they are not touching and bake for 8 to 10 minutes.

EGGPLANT STUFFED WITH VEGETABLES

Choose a firm eggplant that is deep purple and free of scars.

PREPARATION TIME 30 MINUTES   MAKES 3 CUPS

- 1 $1/2$-pound eggplant
- Fresh lemon juice

Wash and cut eggplant lengthwise. Scoop out eggplant flesh (a grapefruit spoon works well), leaving eggplant shell with about $1/2$-inch rim of flesh. Brush shells with lemon juice and set aside. Steam eggplant flesh over 1 cup of water for 7 to 9 minutes.

1   large onion, finely chopped
1   tablespoon finely minced garlic
2   cups diced zucchini
1   cup chopped shiitake mushrooms
2   tomatoes, chopped
1   green pepper, finely chopped
1   red pepper, finely chopped
2   tablespoons extra-virgin olive oil

While eggplant is steaming, use a food processor to cut the above vegetables. Each vegetable should be finely diced but not pureed.

In a large skillet, sauté onion and peppers in oil on medium heat until peppers are soft. Add tomatoes and garlic and continue to cook for a few minutes. Put the cooked vegetables in bowl and set aside. Add a little oil to the skillet and sauté the mushrooms and zucchini for a few minutes. Add the steamed eggplant. Return onion, pepper, tomato, and garlic mixture to the skillet and cook a few more minutes.

$2^1/2$ tablespoons minced fresh parsley
$1/8$ teaspoon chili powder
$1/2$ teaspoon dried thyme
$1/2$ teaspoon dried oregano
$1/2$ teaspoon dried basil

Add spices to the vegetables and mix well. Put the vegetable mixture into the eggplant shells and serve with crisp pita pieces.

HOT MUSHROOMS

Quickly sautéed mushrooms are an elegant appetizer. Use only those that are very fresh and white, wipe them clean with a damp paper towel, and trim stem ends. Mushrooms must not be wet when you add them to the oil or butter. They take only a few minutes and should be served immediately.

PREPARATION TIME 10 MINUTES   4 GENEROUS SERVINGS
COOKING TIME 5 TO 10 MINUTES

2   tablespoons extra-virgin olive oil or unsalted butter
1/2 pound fresh white mushrooms, cleaned and trimmed
1   clove minced garlic
1/4 teaspoon freshly grated nutmeg
     Salt to taste
1   tablespoon fresh lemon juice

In a wide, heavy skillet, heat oil over moderately high heat. Add mushrooms, tossing to coat. Stir in all remaining ingredients *except* the lemon juice. Stirring often, sauté for 5 minutes, or until mushrooms are cooked but still firm. Sprinkle the lemon juice over them and blend in. Serve with picks for spearing.

Note: When mushrooms are sautéed, they immediately absorb the oil; but it comes back, so don't be hasty in adding more oil.

RIPE OLIVE-CHILE-CHEESE SNACKS

These savory, crunchy morsels can disappear so quickly, you might think they evaporated. Cut into wedges, they can serve as appetizers. Or with a bowl of hot soup, they can provide lunch. Canned green chilies vary in size and hotness. Use your judgment after tasting to decide how much of them to include.

PREPARATION TIME 10 MINUTES   4 SERVING OF
BROILING TIME 5 MINUTES   2 HALVES EACH
Preheat broiler.

4   English muffins

Split and toast.

2 to 3 canned green chilies, rinsed, seeded, and chopped
$1/4$ cup low-fat mayonnaise
$2/3$ cup grated low-fat Cheddar cheese
$1/3$ cup mammoth pitted ripe olives, sliced
$1/4$ teaspoon prepared mustard
    Chopped parsley, as desired

Stir together chilies, mayonnaise, cheese, olives, and mustard. Pile equal amounts of the mixture on each muffin half. Place on a cookie sheet and slide the sheet under broiler until cheese melts and mixture is puffed and bubbling. Sprinkle with chopped parsley and serve.

PHYLLO PIZZA

The phyllo dough makes this pizza light and perfect for a delicious appetizer.

PREPARATION TIME 20 MINUTES   MAKES 14 PIZZA STRIPS
BAKING TIME 20 MINUTES
Preheat oven to 375°.

> 1   28-ounce can peeled whole tomatoes

Drain tomatoes, chop coarsely, and drain again.

> 1   medium onion, chopped
> 1   large clove garlic, minced
> 2   tablespoons chopped fresh parsley
> 1   tablespoon extra-virgin olive oil

Over low heat, sauté onions, garlic, and parsley in olive oil. Add drained tomatoes and continue to cook on low heat while working on the dough.

> 8   sheets phyllo dough
> 1   egg white
> 2   tablespoons extra-virgin olive oil

Beat egg white with olive oil. Spray a 10-by-15-inch cookie sheet with oil and top with the phyllo dough, brushing each sheet with the egg white–oil mixture before topping with the next sheet. Tuck the edges under. Spread the tomato mixture evenly on the phyllo.

> 1   cup shredded part-skim mozzarella cheese
> 1/2   cup freshly grated Parmesan cheese
>   Oregano or basil, fresh or dried, to taste

Sprinkle the cheeses and herbs onto the tomato mixture and bake for 20 minutes. Cool. Cut in half lengthwise and then across in 2-inch strips.

PHYLLO WITH POTATO, ONION, AND DILL

Phyllo dough is traditionally prepared with butter—and lots of it on every sheet. This appetizer, like the Phyllo Pizza, has less fat because the dough is brushed with an extra-virgin olive oil and egg white mixture, which gives you the same light and crispy results.

PREPARATION TIME 25 MINUTES   **MAKES 14 PHYLLO STRIPS**
BAKING TIME 20 MINUTES
Preheat oven to 400°.

    4   small boiling potatoes

Peel potatoes but do not cut them. Cover potatoes with lightly salted water and boil until tender.

    8   sheets phyllo dough
    1   egg white
    2   tablespoons extra-virgin olive oil

While potatoes are cooking, beat egg white with the oil. Spray a 10-by-15-inch cookie sheet with oil and top with the phyllo dough, brushing each sheet with the egg white–oil mixture before topping with the next sheet. Tuck the edges under.

    1   onion
    2   tablespoons extra-virgin olive oil
        Dill, fresh or dried, to taste
        Salt and pepper to taste

Cut onion into slices and then separate into rings. Slice the cooked potatoes and place the slices in a single layer on the phyllo dough. Add a layer of onion rings and dribble the olive oil over the topping. Sprinkle with dill and salt and pepper. Bake for 20 minutes. Cut in half lengthwise and then across in 2-inch strips.

STUFFED MUSHROOMS WITH SPINACH AND TOFU

This delightfully light and healthy appetizer will be a crowd pleaser. Serve warm.

PREPARATION TIME 15 MINUTES   **MAKES 24 MUSHROOMS**
BAKING TIME 30 MINUTES
Preheat oven to 375°.
Spray a shallow baking dish with oil.

- 24 medium-sized stuffing mushrooms
- 2 cloves garlic, minced
- 1 tablespoon extra-virgin olive oil

Wipe mushrooms clean with a damp paper towel and remove the stems. Place mushrooms in the oil-sprayed baking dish and set aside. Chop stems and sauté with chopped garlic in oil for 4 minutes.

- 1 10-ounce package frozen spinach, thawed and drained
- 1/2 cup tofu, mashed
- 1 tablespoon freshly grated Parmesan cheese
- 3 tablespoons coarsely chopped walnuts
- 1/4 teaspoon dried thyme
  Salt and pepper to taste

In a medium-sized bowl, mix spinach with tofu, Parmesan cheese, walnuts, thyme, salt, and pepper. Add mushroom stems and garlic.

- 2 tablespoons unsalted butter or margarine, cut into small pieces

Stuff mushrooms with spinach mixture and sprinkle with butter pieces. Bake for 30 minutes until brown and juicy.

TOFU CUBES WITH BASIL

This is a good and nutritious snack. You'll find yourself eating half a plateful while waiting for dinner.

PREPARATION TIME 10 MINUTES   SERVES 4
BAKING TIME 35 MINUTES
Preheat oven to 375°.

    2   teaspoons sesame oil
    1¹/₂ tablespoons reduced-sodium soy sauce
    1¹/₂ tablespoons water

Combine these ingredients in a 9-inch glass baking dish.

    16 ounces tofu, rinsed, dried, and cut into ¹/₂-inch cubes
    1   tablespoon fresh basil, minced

Mix tofu cubes in the dressing, covering evenly. Make sure tofu is in one layer in the baking dish and sprinkle with basil. Bake for 35 minutes, turning 2 or 3 times.

CALZONE

Calzone is a relative of the ubiquitous pizza. It is, in fact, a puffy turnover made with pizza dough. Since calzone is meant to be eaten in the hand, it is excellent for snacks, picnics, and informal entertaining. This version has a light, fluffy filling made with ricotta and egg, but the possibilities for other stuffings are endless. Already prepared pizza dough can be purchased at most supermarkets and pizzerias; we recommend a mostly white dough. To add a nice flavor and color to the dough, try punching in 2 tablespoons minced fresh herbs or 1 tablespoon dried herbs (oregano, basil, chives, sage, or thyme).

PREPARATION TIME 20 MINUTES   SERVES 6
BAKING TIME 20 MINUTES
Preheat oven to 425°.

> 1   **pound pizza dough (purchased, or see recipe on page 165)**

Divide dough into 6 equal pieces (or more for miniature calzone). Form each piece into a ball and roll or pat each ball into a 6- or 7-inch circle.

> 1   **egg, slightly beaten**
> 1   **cup part-skim ricotta cheese**
> ¹/₄ **cup freshly grated Parmesan cheese**
> ¹/₄ **cup chopped parsley**
>   **Pinch of nutmeg**

In a large bowl, thoroughly mix the egg, ricotta, Parmesan, parsley, and nutmeg. Place several tablespoons of this mixture in the center of each round of dough, dividing the amount of filling equally.

> ¹/₂ to ²/₃ **cup shredded part-skim mozzarella cheese**

Sprinkle mozzarella over the filling, moisten the edge of the dough circles with water and fold in half to enclose. Press down the edges and crimp to seal securely.

> **Extra-virgin olive oil**

Place calzone on an oil-sprayed baking sheet, brush the top of each turnover lightly with oil, and bake for 15 to 20 minutes, or until puffy and toasted around the edges.

QUESADILLAS

In Mexico, one of the most popular snacks is the quesadilla. It is a little turnover made with a tortilla and can have a variety of fillings. Our favorite is stuffed with green chilies and Jack cheese. If the tortillas are dry, they must be softened by heat before they are folded over the filling. To do this, pat the tortillas with dampened hands and place them on a moderately hot griddle, turning them until they are soft and warm, about 30 seconds. If left on the heat too long, they will become brittle and impossible to use for quesadillas.

PREPARATION TIME 10 MINUTES   SERVES 6
BAKING TIME 10 MINUTES

> 2 canned green chilies
> 1/2 pound Jack cheese, cut into thick strips
> 6 corn tortillas (available in supermarkets)

Rinse the chilies under cold running water, washing out the seeds. Drain on paper towels and cut into thin strips. Place a strip of cheese and as many strips of chile as you wish in the center of each tortilla, fold over, and place on a medium-hot, griddle that has been lightly sprayed with oil. You may have to hold the folded edge of the tortilla in position with tongs until it has baked a minute or two. When lightly browned on one side, turn quesadilla to other side until browned and the cheese melted.

Crackers

What could be better than a basket of crunchy, homemade crackers still warm and fresh from the oven? Making crackers is so much fun, and so quick and easy to do, that you may never again want to go back to the store-bought variety. And they don't contain a trace of chemical additives!

A food processor makes for speed and ease in mixing ingredients and forming dough in all the cracker recipes in this section.

CRACKED WHEAT WAFERS

PREPARATION TIME 20 MINUTES
BAKING TIME 10 TO 15 MINUTES
Preheat oven to 350°.

MAKES ABOUT 24 WAFERS

1	cup unbleached all-purpose flour
1	teaspoon baking powder
$^1/_2$	teaspoon salt
$^1/_4$	cup cracked wheat
$^1/_4$	teaspoon poppy seeds

Mix flour, baking powder, and salt in a large bowl. (A moment's whirl in food processor will also do the job.) Stir in cracked wheat and poppy seeds.

2	tablespoons cold unsalted butter
$^1/_2$	cup ice water (or less)

In a processor, cut butter into flour mixture until well blended. Quickly but lightly stir in as much water as you need to make a dough that holds together. (This is more easily done in food processor.) Divide dough into two parts, and form each into a ball.

Pat each ball into a rectangle on a lightly floured board and, with a rolling pin, roll out to tissue thinness. Cut with a 2-inch biscuit cutter. Bake wafers on an ungreased cookie sheet for about 10 minutes, or until crisp. Do not allow them to scorch. Cool on a rack and store in an airtight container.

WHEAT WAFERS WITH POPPY SEEDS

PREPARATION TIME 15 MINUTES
BAKING TIME 10 TO 15 MINUTES
Preheat oven to 350°.

MAKES ABOUT 30 WAFERS

$1^1/_2$ cups whole wheat flour
$^1/_2$ cup soy flour
$^1/_2$ teaspoon salt
1 teaspoon baking powder
1 tablespoon poppy seeds

Mix dry ingredients well with a fork.

$^1/_4$ cup canola oil
$^1/_2$ cup ice water (or less)

Blend in oil and add enough water to make dough. Divide dough into 4 parts and roll each paper thin. Cut with a 2-inch biscuit cutter. Bake on ungreased cookie sheet for 10 to 15 minutes, until golden and crisp. Cool on a rack and store in an airtight container.

CHAPATTI CHIPS

PREPARATION TIME 10 MINUTES   MAKES ABOUT 24 CHIPS
BAKING TIME 5 MINUTES

- ¹/₂ cup unprocessed bran
- 1   cup whole wheat flour
- ¹/₄ cup finely chopped toasted sunflower seeds
- 2   tablespoons cold, unsalted butter, cut in small pieces

Combine dry ingredients in a large bowl and add the butter. Mix well with the fingers until crumbly (or use a food processor).

¹/₂ to ²/₃ cup water

Slowly dribble in enough water and knead to form a smooth ball of dough. On a lightly floured surface, roll dough out very thin and cut with a 2-inch biscuit cutter or small jar cover. (Or divide dough into 24 parts and roll each into a marble; then flatten between palms to desired thickness.) Bake on a hot, ungreased griddle until crisp, turning several times during baking. Cool and store airtight.

Note: ¹/₂ teaspoon salt may be added to the dough, but when Chapatti Chips are eaten with cheese, lack of salt is not noticeable.

SESAME SNAPS

PREPARATION TIME 15 MINUTES
BAKING TIME 10 MINUTES
Preheat oven to 350°.

MAKES ABOUT 20 CRACKERS

$1^{1}/_{2}$ cups rye flour
$^{1}/_{4}$ cup soy flour or all-purpose flour
$^{1}/_{4}$ cup raw or toasted sesame seeds
$^{3}/_{4}$ teaspoon salt
1   teaspoon baking powder

Stir together flours, seeds, salt, and baking powder, mixing well.

$^{1}/_{4}$ cup canola oil
$^{1}/_{2}$ cup ice water (or less)

Dribble in oil and blend well. Add water, tossing with a fork (or use a processor) until mixture is of doughlike consistency.

Form into a ball and divide into 4 parts. Roll each tissue thin on a lightly floured board. Cut with a 2-inch biscuit cutter. Bake on an ungreased cookie sheet until crisp, about 10 minutes. Cool on rack and store in an airtight container.

Spreads and Dips

The most important thing to remember about spreads and dips is that they should have a good consistency—not so thin that they drip, nor so thick that they are hard to scoop or spread.

Leftovers make wonderful appetizer spreads. A cup or two of cooked vegetables, with a few additions, can be whirled in a food processor or blender to a smooth, colorful pâté, and no one will guess that it was left from last night's dinner. Here are a few combinations that may suggest still others to you.

DUXELLES

Duxelles is a versatile, exciting substance created by the French. It can be used in so many ways that it is difficult to know just where it belongs in this book. However, since it makes a beautifully simple yet sophisticated appetizer when spread on thin toast or crackers, we decided to put it here. (See page 25 for a further discussion of duxelles.)

PREPARATION TIME 15 MINUTES   MAKES ABOUT 1 CUP
COOKING TIME 8 TO 10 MINUTES

   ¹/₂   pound fresh mushrooms, washed and dried

Finely mince the mushrooms by hand or in a food processor. Gather the mushrooms, a few tablespoons at a time, into the corner of a double thickness of cheesecloth or other clean cloth and twist very hard to extract the juice into a small bowl. (Save this liquid for use in soups, sauces, or cooking vegetables.)

   2   tablespoons unsalted butter
   2   tablespoons minced shallots or scallions

Melt the butter in a large, heavy-bottomed skillet over moderately high heat. Add mushrooms and shallots or scallions and cook, stirring often, until the mushrooms are lightly browned and the liquid disappears.

       Salt and pepper to taste

Add salt and pepper. Allow the mixture to cool. Place the duxelles in a tightly covered glass jar and refrigerate or freeze.

NUT BUTTERS

With the help of a food processor, you can make your own nut butters. In addition to the familiar peanut butter, you can produce smooth, exotic-tasting spreads from almonds, cashews, hazelnuts, walnuts, macadamia nuts, and so on. Butters may be made from raw or roasted nuts, salted or unsalted.

Process up to 2 cups of nuts, stopping occasionally to scrape down the container as the nuts climb up its sides. As the processing continues, the nuts will form a paste that gathers itself into a ball, whirls briefly around the container, and then disperses. At this point, stop the motor and scrape down the container. If the consistency is not smooth enough, continue processing until desired texture is reached. The longer the nut paste is processed, the smoother it will become as oils are released. If the butter remains too dry (some nuts are oilier than others), blend in a tablespoon of canola oil. Salt may be added if you wish. The butter should be refrigerated.

RAW MUSHROOM SPREAD

The subtle, wild taste of raw mushrooms is tantalizing when captured as a spread on toasted whole wheat bread or crisp whole-grain crackers.

PREPARATION TIME 10 MINUTES   **MAKES ABOUT 1 CUP**

    1   8-ounce package light cream cheese
    1   tablespoon chopped chives

In mixer, food processor, or by hand, beat cream cheese and chives together until smooth and creamy.

    1¼ cups finely chopped fresh mushrooms
         Salt to taste
    2   tablespoons minced parsley

Stir in mushrooms and add salt. Mound in small serving bowl and sprinkle with parsley or another fresh herb.

EGGPLANT BUCHAREST

The taste of this dish is like that of no other. And it takes very little work and time to produce it. In selecting your eggplant, pick one that is young, fresh-looking, and has a shiny, unblemished skin. This dish has Middle Eastern origins. There are many versions. A friend who lives in Bucharest, the capital of Romania, told us that it's as popular there as pizza is here.

PREPARATION TIME 10 MINUTES   MAKES ABOUT 1½ CUPS
BROILING TIME 20 MINUTES
Preheat broiler.

1   **medium-sized eggplant**

Wash eggplant but don't cut off ends or peel. Poke a few holes in it with a large fork (so it won't explode in the oven), and place it in a pan under the broiler. Broil for 20 minutes, or until the skin is well charred and the pulp is *very* soft. When cool enough to handle, peel back the skin; and with a large spoon, scoop the pulp out into a small bowl. With the same spoon, chop and stir the pulp until the consistency is smooth and uniform.

½   **teaspoon salt**
¼   **teaspoon freshly ground black pepper**
1 to 2 tablespoons extra-virgin olive oil (optional)
⅓   **cup finely chopped onion**
1   **tablespoon sesame seeds**

Add above ingredients to pulp and blend with a spoon or fork.

Note: Eggplant Bucharest may be served at room temperature or chilled. It is delicious on wheat crackers or toasted rye rounds as an appetizer; it also makes a delightful salad topping on crisp, cold lettuce leaves and slices of avocado and tomato. We often toss in some sliced radishes for lively color and crunch. Sliced ripe olives are a good addition, too.

CARROT PÂTÉ

MICROWAVE

This appetizer is rich in vitamin A. Try spreading the pâté on Cracked Wheat Wafers (see page 46) or Wheat Wafers with Poppy Seeds (see page 47), or crisp, raw vegetables.

PREPARATION TIME 15 MINUTES
COOKING TIME 10 MINUTES

MAKES ABOUT 1½ CUPS

1 tablespoon unsalted butter or margarine
¼ cup sliced or chopped onion
1 clove garlic, minced
½ teaspoon curry powder

Melt the butter or margarine in a heavy pan over moderately low heat. Add the onion and garlic and cook slowly until soft and limp, stirring occasionally. Stir in curry powder and cook a few more seconds. Place in blender or food processor bowl.

1¾ cups chopped carrots
6 tablespoons cashew butter (see Nut Butters, page 51)
Salt (optional)

Place the carrots in a covered container and microwave on High until tender, about 3 to 5 minutes. Add carrots and cashew butter to onion mixture and process until smooth. Taste for seasoning; add salt if needed.

¼ cup coarsely chopped cashews

Stir in chopped cashews. Serve at room temperature. If made ahead, cover and chill. Bring to room temperature before serving.

PEANUT DIP

This spicy dip is an irresistible companion to colorful, sliced raw vegetables, such as sweet peppers, small Kirby cucumbers, crunchy sugar snap peas and bright, crisp carrots. It's great, too, with corn chips. Make plenty; it disappears quickly.

PREPARATION TIME 15 MINUTES   MAKES 1½ CUPS

    ¹/₄ cup dry-roasted peanuts

Coarsely chop peanuts by hand or in a food processor.

    1 cup peanut butter (lightly salted, no sugar added)
    1 tablespoon minced fresh ginger
    1 tablespoon minced garlic
    3 tablespoons Oriental sesame oil
    2 tablespoons rice vinegar
    3 tablespoons vegetable broth
    ¹/₂ teaspoon Oriental hot oil (chile oil)

Blend above ingredients in food processor until well mixed. Add the coarsely chopped nuts and process just long enough to distribute them.

    ¹/₄ cup chopped fresh cilantro

Scoop peanut dip into serving bowl and sprinkle with cilantro.

Note: Peanut butter varies in dryness. This mixture may need to be thinned a little with more broth. It should not, however, be so thin that it drips off dipped vegetables.

WHITE BEAN DIP

Topped with cucumber slices, diced tomatoes and shredded cabbage, this dip doubles nicely for a sandwich spread.

PREPARATION TIME 10 MINUTES   MAKES ABOUT 1 CUP

    1¹/₄ cups cooked white beans or chickpeas
    3 tablespoons fresh lemon juice
    2 tablespoons extra-virgin olive oil

Put beans, lemon juice, and oil in container of blender or food processor. Whirl until smooth and blended, stopping the motor occasionally to push the mixture down into the blades. Add a little water if mixture is too thick.

1   small clove garlic, minced
    Salt and pepper to taste

Add garlic, salt, and pepper and blend again. Serve garnished with toasted sesame seeds or pine nuts.

MUSHROOM BUTTER

A bit of nutmeg gives this pale, creamy spread a delicate, intriguing flavor that is very special. For an extra treat, spread it on toasted French bread rounds and slide them under the broiler for a moment or two until bubbly.

PREPARATION TIME 10 MINUTES
COOKING TIME 10 MINUTES   **MAKES ABOUT 1³/₄ CUPS**

2   tablespoons unsalted butter or margarine
¹/₂ cup finely chopped onions
¹/₂ pound fresh mushrooms, thickly sliced

Melt butter in large, heavy frying pan. Add onions and cook over moderately low heat for a few minutes. Add mushrooms, tossing and stirring to coat with butter. Sauté 5 minutes.

¹/₈ teaspoon freshly grated nutmeg
¹/₂ teaspoon salt
1   tablespoon lemon juice
¹/₈ teaspoon freshly ground black pepper
1   tablespoon unsalted butter or margarine

Stir in nutmeg, salt, lemon juice, pepper, and butter. Cook, stirring, until butter melts and seasonings are blended. Place mixture in blender or food processor and blend.

¹/₄ cup freshly grated Parmesan cheese

Add cheese to blender and process again. Scrape mixture into a jar, cover, and chill.

GUACAMOLE

This is a traditional summer favorite. Salt is optional but should be omitted if serving with salted corn chips.

PREPARATION TIME 10 MINUTES   **MAKES ABOUT 1½ CUPS**

2	medium-sized ripe avocados
1½	tablespoons fresh lemon juice
¼	cup minced red onion or scallions
1	tablespoon finely chopped canned green chilies
1	ripe tomato, chopped
1	clove garlic, finely diced
1	tablespoon minced cilantro
⅛	teaspoon salt (optional)

Combine all ingredients in a food processor or blender. Cover guacamole with plastic wrap to keep it from darkening and refrigerate if prepared ahead of time. Stir before serving at room temperature.

Snack Mixtures

Mixtures of dried fruits, nuts, seeds, and cereals are lightweight sources of quick energy for the hiker, biker, student, and office worker. With wine or other beverages, they can also serve as appetizers. Exact amounts and proportions are unimportant in some of these blends. They can all be made in a few minutes.

BACKPACK SNACK

Wheat or rye flakes (available at health food stores)
Raw sunflower seeds
Raw sesame seeds

Toast the flakes, sunflower seeds, and sesame seeds in an ungreased skillet. Pour into a bowl.

Whole or chopped nuts
Raisins
Dried fruits, chopped

Add nuts, raisins, and dried fruits to the bowl. Cool the mixture completely. Carry in tightly closed plastic bags or other containers.

TROPICAL FRUIT AND NUT MIX

Dried pears, chopped
Dates, pitted and chopped
Dried banana chips
Cashew nuts, broken
Coconut, dried, unsweetened
Raisins

Mix all ingredients and package in airtight container.

FLAVORED NUTS AND SEEDS

Highly nutritious nuts and seeds make tasty little nibbles just as they are. For extra flavor and enjoyment, however, toast them in the oven with a blend of spices and other seasonings. Use raw nuts and seeds that have not been previously roasted and salted. English walnuts, pecans, cashews, almonds, peanuts, filberts, and dried, hulled sunflower, pumpkin, and squash seeds all make excellent appetizers when prepared this way.

PREPARATION TIME 10 MINUTES   **MAKES 1 CUP**
TOASTING TIME 13 MINUTES
Preheat oven to 350°.

1   cup shelled nuts or dried seeds

Spread nuts or seeds in a shallow pan in a single layer. Toast in oven until golden, about 10 minutes. Stir often.

1 to 2 teaspoons canola oil

Use the oil with one of the following seasoning mixtures:

Mexican: 1 teaspoon chili powder, $1/2$ teaspoon ground cumin, $1/4$ teaspoon ground coriander, $1/4$ teaspoon salt, dash of cayenne pepper

Indian: $1/2$ teaspoon ground turmeric, $1/4$ teaspoon ground coriander, $1/4$ teaspoon cayenne pepper, $1/4$ teaspoon salt, $1/8$ teaspoon garlic powder

Chinese: $1/2$ teaspoon Chinese five-spice powder, $1/4$ teaspoon salt (or to taste)

Herb: $1/4$ teaspoon each crumbled dried rosemary, thyme, and oregano; $1/2$ teaspoon salt, $1/4$ teaspoon cayenne pepper

Sprinkle the nuts or seeds with oil and stir in one of the seasonings suggested (or your own original blend). Return the mixture to the oven for 3 minutes, stirring to combine flavors well. Let stand to cool and crisp. Store in an airtight container.

Note: English walnuts should be blanched before toasting to remove their astringency. Drop them in boiling water and boil for 3 minutes. Drain and dry on paper towels before proceeding.

CHURA

This is an adaptation of a spicy East Indian snack. We doubt if Indians ever use sunflower seeds in their Chura, and they certainly don't use Rice Krispies, nor would they make it so mild as ours. If you like it hotter, add a dash of cayenne pepper or chili powder.

PREPARATION TIME 10 MINUTES
COOKING TIME 3 MINUTES

MAKES 2 CUPS

2	tablespoons canola oil
1	teaspoon ground coriander
1/2	teaspoon ground cumin
1/2	teaspoon ground turmeric
1/4	teaspoon dry mustard

In a large, heavy frying pan, heat the oil over a moderate flame. Stir in the combined spices and blend into the oil until well heated. Remove pan from heat.

1	cup Rice Krispies
1/2	cup salted Spanish peanuts
1/2	cup roasted cashews
1/3	cup raisins
1/4	cup roasted sunflower seeds
1/4	teaspoon ground cloves

Mix all ingredients and stir into spiced oil to blend the flavors. Allow to cool. This will keep about 1 week if stored in an airtight container. Do not refrigerate.

PEANUT POPCORN

This is a delicious snack for any age, and the peanuts and sunflower seeds boost its nutritional value. Barley malt, a grain sweetener, is stronger in flavor than honey but milder than molasses and works best in Peanut Popcorn, though maple syrup and honey can be substituted with fine results.

PREPARATION TIME 15 MINUTES   **MAKES 12 CUPS OF POPCORN**

PREHEAT OVEN TO 350°.

$1/2$ cup popping corn

Pop corn in a hot-air popcorn maker. Transfer to an extra large bowl, making sure to sift out any unpopped kernels. Set aside.

$1/2$ cup unsalted peanuts
$1/4$ cup sunflower seeds

Lightly toast peanuts and seeds in oven (or toaster oven) for 3 to 5 minutes. Add to the popcorn.

1   tablespoon canola oil
$1/4$ teaspoon curry powder
$1/4$ teaspoon salt
$1/4$ cup barley malt, maple syrup, or honey

In a small saucepan, heat oil over low heat. Add the curry powder and salt and sauté for a few seconds. Raise to medium heat, stir in the barley malt, and cook a few minutes until syrup boils and is bubbly. Pour the hot syrup mixture over the popcorn, peanuts, and seeds and stir well to coat. Let cool completely before storing in an airtight container. Break into clusters to serve. Do not refrigerate.

Sandwiches

In this section, we offer mixtures that can be stuffed in pita bread or between the conventional two pieces of bread.

AVOCADO POCKET SANDWICH

This makes a quick and easy treat for a luncheon buffet, picnic, or even for brown-bagging.

PREPARATION TIME 15 MINUTES   SERVES 4

- 1   ripe avocado, peeled, halved, and seeded
- 1/2 cup chopped cucumber
- 1/2 cup chopped cauliflower
- 1/2 cup sliced mushrooms
- 1/2 cup diced or shredded low-fat Monterey Jack cheese
- 1/4 cup Italian dressing

Dice half the avocado; reserve the other half. Toss diced avocado, cucumber, cauliflower, mushrooms, and cheese with Italian dressing.

- 2   large or 4 small pita breads
- 1   teaspoon fresh lemon juice
- 1/2 cup chopped tomato

Cut the pitas in half if large or slit halfway around the edge and separate if smaller; pull the edges apart to form a pocket. Fill each with 1/4 of the mixture. Mash the remaining avocado with a fork and stir in the lemon juice and tomato. Spoon mixture inside each sandwich.

CURRIED TOFU SALAD SANDWICH

Similar to egg salad but without the eggs, this salad is a delicious alternative. Serve in a pita or on wheat bread with lettuce and tomato.

PREPARATION TIME 10 MINUTES   SERVES 4

1	pound extra firm or firm tofu
1/2	teaspoon curry powder
	Pinch of ground cumin
1/4	cup finely diced carrots
1/4	cup finely diced celery
3	tablespoons low-fat mayonnaise

Rinse tofu and pat dry. In a medium bowl, mash it with a fork until it is the size of small peas. Mix in the curry and cumin. Add carrots, celery, and mayonnaise and stir until blended. Chill.

EGGPLANT, TOFU, AND GRILLED ONION SANDWICH

This delicious sandwich is best made on crusty French bread. It's not bad either in a pita, split and lightly toasted. By roasting the eggplant, instead of frying, we cut down on its oil absorption.

PREPARATION TIME 25 MINUTES   SERVES 4

Preheat oven to 450°.

2	tablespoon extra-virgin olive oil
1	medium eggplant
	Garlic powder
	Onion powder

Peel eggplant and cut crosswise into 1/3-inch slices. Arrange them on a cookie sheet that has been lightly sprayed with oil. Brush each slice with olive oil and sprinkle with a little garlic powder and onion powder. Bake for 10 minutes, turn slices, brush with oil, sprinkle with garlic and onion powder, and bake another 10 minutes.

1   tablespoon extra-virgin olive oil
1   medium mild onion
$1/2$ pound firm tofu
1   tablespoon light soy sauce

While the eggplant is roasting, slice the onion thinly. Cut the tofu into $1/4$-inch slices. Sauté the onion and tofu in olive oil in 12-inch nonstick pan until lightly browned, about 5 minutes. Brush each tofu slice with soy sauce.

French bread or pitas for 4 sandwiches
Dijon mustard
Low-fat mayonnaise

Bread should be warm. Spread half of sandwich with mayo and half with mustard. Add onion, eggplant, and tofu.

SPICY TACO PITA

The spiciness is off-set by the sweetness of raisins in this pita treat. Try it also as a salad (see page 96).

PREPARATION TIME 20 MINUTES   SERVES 6
COOKING TIME 15 MINUTES

4   tablespoons slivered almonds

Place almonds in heavy-bottomed frying pan and toast over moderate heat until golden, shaking pan occasionally. Remove nuts from pan and set aside.

2   tablespoons canola oil
1/4 cup chopped onion

In the same pan, heat the oil and stir in the chopped onion; cook until limp and translucent. Pour off excess fat.

3   cups cooked kidney beans, mashed
1/2 cup tomato sauce
1/2 cup water
2   canned green chilies, rinsed, seeded, and chopped
1/4 cup raisins
1/2 teaspoon dried oregano
1/4 teaspoon ground cumin
     Salt and pepper to taste

To the sautéed onion, add kidney beans, tomato sauce, water, chilies, raisins, oregano, cumin, salt, and pepper and mix well. Cook, stirring, until liquid has evaporated. Fold in the almonds.

1   cup diced or shredded Jack cheese
2   cups shredded lettuce
     Tomato slices, halved
3   large pita breads, halved

Arrange cheese, lettuce, and tomato slices in separate bowls. Spoon the hot bean mixture into the pita pockets and top with cheese, lettuce, and tomato.

Soups

Aeons ago someone said, "A soup—to be good—has to be cooked slowly and for a long, long time." This was then repeated endlessly. Someone also put that same thought in writing, and it was copied diligently by scribes. Thus myths are created.

Despite this, our soup recipes emphasize speed and ease of preparation. We also have our sights set on soups that are nutritious, and therefore healthful, as well as delicious. Richness of flavor and aroma are achieved with herbs and spices and vegetable stock.

BEAN AND VEGETABLE SOUP

You can use almost any kind of bean. This soup is especially delicious served with warm, crusty French bread.

PREPARATION TIME 15 MINUTES   SERVES 8 TO 10
COOKING TIME 25 MINUTES

3	large carrots
3	large onions
3	stalks celery
3	cups cooked beans
	Water, as needed (approximately 9 cups)

If you use canned beans, rinse and drain. Cut the carrots, onions, and celery in pieces that are large but easy to process.

Put a fistful of the vegetables and beans in processor and almost cover with water. Process very briefly, just long enough to make a thick purée. Pour into a large pot. You will have to repeat the procedure a couple of times to do all the vegetables and beans. Simmer purée in the pot for about 20 minutes.

> 1 to 2 cups pasta, (spaghetti broken in small pieces, elbow macaroni, or any pasta of your choosing)

Place pasta in pot and continue to simmer until it is al dente. Remove from heat.

1	tablespoon nutritional yeast (optional)
1	teaspoon miso, softened in 1 tablespoon of warm water
1	teaspoon dried basil

Stir thoroughly into soup. Serve while hot. When it is necessary to reheat the soup, do not boil.

BEET SOUP

This soup may not have the authenticity of the steppes of Russia, but it evokes crusty black bread and other sturdy, nutritious, peasant fare.

PREPARATION TIME 15 MINUTES   SERVES 4 TO 6
COOKING TIME 3 MINUTES

- 2   cups canned beets
- 2   carrots
- 1   medium onion
- 1   cup shredded cabbage
- 3   cups vegetable broth or water
- $^1/_2$ teaspoon salt
  Few turns of pepper grinder
- 2   tablespoons unsalted butter
- 1   tablespoon fresh lemon juice
  Light sour cream or nonfat yogurt (optional)

Cut up vegetables coarsely and, except for the beets, put them in a pressure cooker along with the broth, salt, pepper, butter, and lemon juice. Cook for 3 minutes. Put half of the cooked vegetables and beets in food processor with 1 cup of broth from the pressure cooker. Blend for 30 seconds. Return to pressure cooker and keep on low heat. Serve with topping of light sour cream or nonfat yogurt.

BLACK-EYED PEA SOUP

A very hearty soup, but good in hot as well as cold weather.

PREPARATION TIME 15 MINUTES   SERVES 6
COOKING TIME 1 HOUR

- 1   cup dried black-eyed peas

Rinse until clean.

- 4   good-sized carrots, cut in $^1/_8$-inch slices
- 1   large onion, chopped
- 2   stalks celery, cut in $^1/_8$-inch slices
- 2   tablespoons extra-virgin olive oil
- 8   cups water

Place above ingredients in pot with black-eyed peas. Cook uncovered at fast simmer until peas start to become soft, about 50 minutes. Cover at this point so no more water evaporates.

$^1/_2$ cup red, white, and green pasta spirals

Add to pot and simmer until tender. Then remove pot from heat.

1 tablespoon nutritional yeast (optional)
1 teaspoon miso, softened in a few tablespoons of cooking liquid
1 teaspoon reduced-sodium soy sauce

Put in pot and stir until well mixed. May be reheated, but do not boil.

BROCCOLI-CHEESE SOUP

Kids who won't eat their vegetables will like this soup, a subtle, creamy blend of vegetables and cheese. After that, Bananas Praline for dessert (see page 216).

PREPARATION TIME 25 MINUTES   SERVES 4
COOKING TIME 15 MINUTES

2 cups potatoes, cut in pieces (about 2 medium potatoes)
$1^1/_2$ cups chopped carrots (about 3 to 4 carrots)
2 cups chopped broccoli
3 cloves garlic
1 cup chopped onion
$^1/_2$ teaspoon salt (optional)
$3^1/_2$ cups water

In a soup pot, bring the above ingredients to a boil, cover, and simmer for 15 minutes. Purée the mixture in a food processor or blender and return soup to pot.

$1^1/_4$ cups grated low-fat cheese
$1^1/_2$ cups low-fat or skim milk
Pinch of dried dill or basil
Freshly ground pepper to taste

Stir in cheese and milk and season to taste.

CARROT SOUP

Smooth as a shake, this soup calls for the help of both a pressure cooker and a food processor or blender. They work wonderfully as a team.

PREPARATION TIME 15 MINUTES   SERVES 4
COOKING TIME 5 MINUTES

> 4   large carrots
> 1   medium onion
> 1   stalk celery
> 1   cup water

Cut carrots lengthwise down the center and then cut these two pieces in half crosswise. Quarter the onion and slice celery in several large pieces. Put vegetables in pressure cooker with water. Cook for 3 minutes. Place in processor or blender.

> $1/2$ cup cooked brown rice
> 1   cup low-fat milk
> 1   teaspoon salt
> Freshly ground pepper to taste

Add these ingredients to the contents of processor or blender. Blend until smooth, about 30 seconds. Return mixture to pressure cooker.

> 2   tablespoons unsalted butter

Add butter. Heat on low to medium heat in uncovered pressure cooker. This soup can also be served cold.

CORN CHOWDER

A classic recipe in a form that meets today's nutritional standards.

PREPARATION TIME 20 MINUTES   SERVES 4
COOKING TIME 30 MINUTES

> 3   cups water
> $1/2$ cup diced onion
> $1/2$ cup diced celery
> 1   cup diced potatoes (about 1 medium potato)

In a soup pot, simmer until the potatoes are cooked, about 15 minutes.

    1   teaspoon dried dill
    1½ cups corn, fresh or frozen

Add to pot and cook a few more minutes.

    2   cups low-fat milk
    1   tablespoon unsalted butter

Add the milk and butter. Don't allow soup to boil.

    4   ounces light cream cheese
    1   tablespoon nutritional yeast (optional)

Take 1 cup of soup and blend in food processor or blender with cream cheese and yeast. Return to the pot and heat until warmed through.

COLD CUCUMBER-MINT SOUP

A refreshing soup when the weather is hot, mild, or even chilly.

PREPARATION TIME 20 MINUTES   SERVES 4 TO 6
CHILLING TIME IN FREEZER 30 MINUTES

    1   tablespoon unsalted butter
    1   cup finely chopped onion
    1   large garlic clove, minced
    4   Kirby cucumbers, unpeeled, thinly sliced

In large skillet, melt butter over medium heat, add onion and garlic, and sauté for 3 minutes. Add cucumber slices and continue sautéing until soft.

    2   tablespoons finely chopped fresh mint or 1 teaspoon dried
    2   cups vegetable broth (from powder or cube)

Add broth, bring to a boil, reduce heat, and simmer for 5 minutes. Pour into food processor and purée. Place in a bowl, stir in mint, cover, and chill well.

    2   cups nonfat plain yogurt
        Salt and pepper to taste
    1   Kirby cucumber (unpeeled), sliced

Just before serving, stir in yogurt and blend well. Add salt and pepper as desired. Garnish each serving with a cucumber slice or two or three.

CURRIED PEA SOUP

A beautiful, pastel-green soup that's fragrant and delicious.

PREPARATION TIME 15 MINUTES   SERVES 4
COOKING TIME 5 MINUTES

- 1   cup fresh or frozen peas
- 1   medium onion, quartered
- 1   medium carrot, cut lengthwise
- 1   clove garlic
- 1   stalk celery with leaves
- 1   medium potato, peeled and quartered
- $1/2$ teaspoon salt
- 1   teaspoon curry powder
- 3   tablespoons unsalted butter
- 1   cup vegetable broth or water

Cook all ingredients in pressure cooker for 2 minutes and then put them in a food processor or blender. Blend for 10 seconds.

- 1   cup low-fat milk
- 1   cup water
       Minced parsley

While the processor is still running, pour in milk and water. After 20 seconds, pour the mixture into the pressure cooker. Heat on medium heat without the cover. Serve with garnish of minced parsley.

CURRY SOUP (WITH ANY VEGETABLE)

We usually make this cold soup with zucchini, but you can use broccoli, corn, tomatoes, carrots, or whatever vegetable you wish.

PREPARATION TIME 15 MINUTES   SERVES 8
CHILLING TIME 30 MINUTES

- 6 to 8 cups chopped zucchini (or other vegetable)
- $3/4$ cup chopped onion
- $3/4$ cup chopped scallion

3   cloves garlic, minced
1   tablespoon chopped fresh ginger
3 to 4 teaspoons curry powder
1   quart vegetable broth
    Salt and pepper to taste

Simmer ingredients until vegetables are tender. Put in food processor and purée. Chill.

1   cup nonfat plain yogurt

Put 1 generous tablespoon of yogurt atop each bowlful when serving.

GAZPACHO FAVORITE

Our family has been making this cold soup for over a generation. It's a favorite. We always make some in the fall when tomatoes are plentiful and at their best. It's a great time-saver because you make 4 quarts at a time and freeze them and each quart serves 4 to 6. Cucumbers, garlic, and tomato juice are added at serving time to give this delightful soup a truly fresh taste.

PREPARATION TIME 30 MINUTES   SERVES 4 TO 6 PER QUART

24 medium-sized tomatoes, coarsely chopped
2 or 3 7-ounce jars roasted red peppers, chopped
6   cups chopped mild onion
1/2 cup extra-virgin olive oil
1/2 cup balsamic vinegar or red wine vinegar

Stir above ingredients together well and freeze in quart containers.

4   cups low-sodium tomato juice
2   Kirby cucumbers (unpeeled), diced
1   large clove garlic, minced
1/4 teaspoon Tabasco (or to taste)
    Salt and pepper to taste

When ready to serve, partially defrost a container and add the above ingredients. Serve in chilled bowls; add ice cubes if soup is entirely thawed.

THE GRAND LEFTOVER SOUP

Any combination of leftovers works. And just about all you need do is blend them with milk and seasonings.

PREPARATION TIME 10 MINUTES   SERVES 4
COOKING TIME 15 TO 20 MINUTES

    1   medium onion, chopped
    1   tablespoon canola oil or unsalted butter
    1/2 cup vegetable broth or water

Sauté onion in oil or butter in large, heavy saucepan over low to medium heat until tender. Add broth or water and cook for 3 minutes.

    1   cup leftover vegetables
    1   cup low-fat milk

Add vegetables and milk to cooked onion, put in food processor, and blend until smooth. Pour back into saucepan.

    1 1/2 cups vegetable broth or water

Add broth or water to vegetables in saucepan and simmer for 5 to 10 minutes.

Note: You don't need to use precisely 1 cup of vegetables. If you use more, you can always correct consistency, if necessary, by adding more milk. Include legumes if you wish. Cooked potatoes and/or cooked brown rice add body to the soup.

HOT WEATHER TOFU BORSCHT

Borscht traditionally comes hot or cold, with or without a boiled potato, and almost inevitably with sour cream. This cold beet soup, a beautiful shade of pink, comes without the potato and without the sour cream.

PREPARATION TIME 15 MINUTES   SERVES 4

    1/2 pound soft tofu
    2   tablespoons canola oil
    4   tablespoons fresh lemon juice
    1/2 teaspoon salt

In a food processor or blender, combine all the ingredients. Empty into bowl and refrigerate while doing the next step.

    ¹/₃ cup onion, chopped
    1¹/₄ cups canned beets
    2   teaspoons prepared horseradish (more or less to taste)

In the processor or blender, mix onions, beets, and horseradish. Add tofu mixture.

    1   cup crushed ice

Add ice and blend well. Serve very cold.

MISO SOUP

This soothing soup is just right for a rainy day. It's light and easy to prepare. Miso soup also works well as an appetizer to a hearty meal.

PREPARATION TIME 10 MINUTES   **SERVES 4**
COOKING TIME 30 MINUTES

    2   teaspoons Oriental sesame oil
    ¹/₃ cup diced carrots
    ¹/₃ cup diced green pepper
    2   scallions, white part only, diced

Heat oil in the bottom of a soup pot and sauté the vegetables for 10 minutes.

    4   cups water
    ¹/₄ pound tofu, cut in ¹/₂-inch cubes

Add water and tofu and simmer for 10 minutes.

         Small handful of spaghetti or Japanese noodles, broken into
         2-inch pieces
    2   tablespoons miso

Add noodles to pot and simmer for 10 minutes. Take 1 cup of the soup liquid and allow it to cool before dissolving miso in it. Return mixture to pot and stir well to combine. Do not boil.

MUSHROOM AND ONION SOUP

If you like the unique flavor of mushrooms, you'll surely enjoy this soup. The other ingredients enhance the mushroom quality rather than blanket it.

PREPARATION TIME 15 MINUTES   SERVES 2
COOKING TIME 10 MINUTES

    2   tablespoons unsalted butter
    6   medium-sized shiitake or other mushrooms
    1/2 small onion

Melt butter in small skillet. Cut mushrooms and onion into large pieces and sauté for 3 minutes.

    3   cups low-fat milk
    3   tablespoons whole wheat flour
    1/2 teaspoon salt
         Freshly ground pepper
         Grated nutmeg

Put these ingredients, in the order given, into the processor or blender. Add sautéed mushrooms and onions. Blend until smooth, about 30 seconds. Pour mixture into a saucepan and heat. When soup has reached simmering stage, reduce heat to low. It can stay on this heat while the rest of the meal is being prepared.

ONION-CHEESE SOUP

This soup amounts to a cheese sandwich in liquid form. It's easy and delicious.

PREPARATION TIME 15 MINUTES   SERVES 3 GENEROUSLY
COOKING TIME 15 MINUTES

    2   medium onions, finely chopped
    2   tablespoons unsalted butter
    2   tablespoons whole wheat flour

Sauté onions in butter in large, heavy saucepan for 3 minutes. Stir in flour thoroughly to make a roux.

    1 1/2 cups water

Gradually, add water to the roux stirring all the while. Simmer for 5 minutes.

1¹/₂ cups low-fat milk
¹/₂   teaspoon salt
      Freshly ground pepper to taste

Add milk and seasonings to saucepan and bring to a boil.

1   cup coarsely grated low-fat Cheddar cheese

Stir cheese into hot mixture until it dissolves.

2   slices whole wheat toast, buttered
      Minced parsley

Place one piece of toast on top of the other. Cut the toast into narrow strips, and then cut across them to make croutons. Put equal amounts of croutons into three bowls. Ladle soup over croutons, sprinkle with parsley, and serve.

PIZZA SOUP
(A "pizza" you eat with a spoon)

This recipe isn't a substitute for pizza; it merely suggests pizza. It's so hearty that some may regard it as almost a complete meal.

PREPARATION TIME 20 MINUTES   SERVES 6
COOKING TIME 12 MINUTES

2	tablespoons unsalted butter
1	medium onion, chopped
2	stalks celery, chopped
1	clove garlic, minced

Sauté vegetables in butter for 3 minutes.

1	cup elbow macaroni

Cook according to package directions, but don't overcook. Drain and set aside.

3	cups vegetable broth or water
2	cups cooked lima beans (cooked frozen limas may be used)
3	tablespoons tomato paste

Combine with sautéed ingredients in a saucepan.

1	carrot (cut into chunks)
1	cup cooked lima beans
1	cup vegetable broth or water

Put in food processor and blend. Mix with other ingredients in saucepan and bring to a simmer.

4 to 6	sliced mushrooms
$1/2$	teaspoon salt
	Freshly ground pepper to taste
$1/4$ to 1	teaspoon dried oregano
	Grated Parmesan cheese or slivered part-skim mozzarella
	Nutritional yeast (optional)

Add mushrooms, seasonings, and reserved macaroni to the soup. Serve topped with Parmesan cheese or mozzarella and a sprinkling of nutritional yeast. If you use mozzarella, cut it in thin slivers (this is best done with an electric knife). Another way is to blend mozzarella and pieces of whole wheat bread in blender. The cheese is easier to handle in this form, since slivers of mozzarella tend to stick together.

SPLIT PEA SOUP

Of the various split pea soups we make, this is the simplest and easiest. No celery. No onions. Simply split peas, potatoes, butter, salt, a sprinkling of dillweed, and oregano.

PREPARATION TIME 10 MINUTES   SERVES 6 TO 8
COOKING TIME 45 MINUTES

    $1/2$ **pound split peas**

Wash peas by putting them in a large mixing bowl and swirling them quickly with one hand, around and around, as cold water runs into the bowl from the faucet. Pour water off and repeat swirling process until peas appear a bright, clean green. (All legumes can be cleaned effectively by this method.)

    $7^1/_2$ **cups vegetable broth or water or a combination**
    $1/2$ **teaspoon salt (if needed)**

Put broth and salt in soup pot, add split peas, and bring to a boil. Reduce heat and cook for about 25 minutes.

    2   **medium potatoes**

Peel potatoes, cut into chunks, and add to pot. Continue cooking for another 20 minutes or so.

    1   **tablespoon unsalted butter**
        Fresh or dried dillweed to taste
        Oregano, to taste

Add butter, dillweed, and oregano to soup 5 to 10 minutes before it is done—that is, when potatoes are soft and split peas have virtually become liquid.

FRESH TOMATO SOUP

When your garden becomes a cornucopia of tomatoes, make this soup. We've even found it to be good using supermarket winter tomatoes that are well ripened.

PREPARATION TIME 10 MINUTES   SERVES 3
COOKING TIME 15 MINUTES

- 1   medium onion, chopped
- 2   tablespoons unsalted butter

Sauté onion in a heavy saucepan until soft.

- 6   tomatoes, sliced
- 2   tablespoons tomato paste
- 1   teaspoon chopped fresh dill
- 3/4 cup vegetable broth or water

Add these ingredients to the sautéed onion and simmer, covered, for 10 minutes.

- 2   teaspoons sugar
       Salt and freshly ground pepper to taste
       Minced fresh dill or basil (optional)

After adding the seasonings, whirl the soup briefly in a food processor or blender. Reheat and serve with a sprinkling of fresh herb.

TOMATO AND RICE SOUP

A remarkably simple soup, it has an astonishingly complex flavor. It's difficult to believe that its base is nothing more than tomato juice.

PREPARATION TIME 10 MINUTES   SERVES 2 GENEROUSLY

- 3   tablespoons chopped onion
- 1   tablespoon unsalted butter

In a saucepan, sauté onions in butter for 3 minutes.

- 3   cups tomato juice
- 1   cup cooked brown rice
- 1/2 cup low-fat milk

Sprinkling of fresh or dried basil
Sugar to taste

Add tomato juice, rice, milk, and seasonings to sautéed onion and heat to simmering point. Remove from heat and serve.

VEGETABLE STEW SOUP

The sort of hearty soup that has special appeal on a cold, blustery day. It can be made very quickly.

PREPARATION TIME 10 MINUTES **SERVES 3**
COOKING TIME 5 MINUTES

2   carrots
1   large onion
1   stalk celery
1   cup vegetable broth or water

Cut vegetables into large pieces and put in pressure cooker. Add liquid and cook for 3 minutes.

1   small green bell pepper, diced
1   cup cooked lima beans (frozen or canned)
1   teaspoon salt

Put these ingredients in food processor or blender with cooked vegetables and blend until smooth. Transfer to pressure cooker.

2   tablespoons unsalted butter
3/4 cup low-fat milk
    Pinch dillweed, chervil, or oregano, or use all three

Mix with ingredients in the pressure cooker. Heat to simmer, uncovered.

ZUCCHINI-YOGURT SOUP

Cold and tangy, this soup is just right on a hot day. What's more, since the yogurt isn't subjected to heat, no harm comes to its friendly, vitamin B–producing bacteria.

PREPARATION TIME 10 MINUTES   **SERVES 4**
COOKING TIME 10 MINUTES
CHILLING TIME 20 TO 30 MINUTES

>1 large onion, chopped
>1 clove garlic, minced
>2 tablespoons unsalted butter

Sauté onion and garlic in butter for 3 minutes.

>2 cups vegetable broth or water
>2 medium zucchini (about 1 pound), diced
>1/2 teaspoon salt
> Freshly ground pepper to taste

Bring broth to a boil in a saucepan. Add sautéed vegetables, zucchini, salt, and pepper. Simmer for 5 minutes.

>1/2 teaspoon curry powder
>1/4 teaspoon dried thyme

Add either or both to soup, according to taste. Cool; then chill soup in freezer for up to 30 minutes.

>2 cups plain low-fat yogurt

When soup is ready to be served, stir in yogurt.

Salads and Salad Dressings

Once, iceberg lettuce was synonymous with salad; an angular chunk of it was positioned in the center of a plate and daubed with mayonnaise or bottled dressing. Now, all sorts of leafy greens are available: romaine, the two Bs (bibb and Boston), escarole, chicory, arugula, watercress, et cetera. And people have come a long way in what they regard as acceptable to enhance the greens: sprouts, tofu, cheese, seeds, nuts, fruits, on and on. What's more, there's no longer a need to use the same old bottled dressings. New ones can be whipped up quickly in a food processor or blender.

AGAR SALAD

Agar, a jelling substance made from seaweed, can be used in salads. There are several forms of agar: bars, granules, flakes, and powder. Salads use the kind packaged in long, thin strips. Though it is tasteless, agar absorbs the flavors of the dressing and adds a slightly chewy texture to the salad. It can be purchased in Oriental food markets and natural food stores.

PREPARATION TIME 15 MINUTES   SERVES 4 AS A SIDE DISH
CHILLING TIME 30 MINUTES

> $^1/_2$ ounce agar, cut in 2-inch strips

Soak agar in cold water for 15 minutes.

> $^1/_2$ head iceberg or romaine (or a combination of the two)
> 1 stalk celery, sliced thin
> 2 radishes, sliced thin
> 1 small cucumber, peeled and sliced thin
> $^1/_2$ cup bean sprouts

While the agar is soaking, cut and toss vegetables in a salad bowl.

> 2 tablespoons reduced-sodium soy sauce
> 2 tablespoons Oriental sesame oil
> $^1/_2$ teaspoon sugar

Combine dressing ingredients in a small bowl or jar and set aside. Drain agar and combine well with the salad. Cover and refrigerate for at least 30 minutes. Pour dressing over salad just before serving.

ANTIPASTO SALAD

Fresh, colorful vegetables lightly cooked in a spicy tomato sauce flavored with herbs and then chilled are a traditional appetizer course in Italy. Served on a bed of lettuce with marinated tofu cubes or an assortment of cheeses, they become a complete-meal salad or the perfect companion to a simple pasta dish.

PREPARATION TIME 20 MINUTES

COOKING TIME 8 TO 10 MINUTES

CHILLING TIME SEVERAL HOURS OR OVERNIGHT

SERVES 4 AS A MAIN COURSE

OR 6 AS A SIDE DISH

2 8-ounce cans tomato sauce
1/2 cup ketchup or chili sauce
1/2 cup extra-virgin olive oil
1/3 cup fresh lemon juice
1 teaspoon dried oregano
1 teaspoon dried basil
2 teaspoons prepared horseradish
1 large clove garlic, crushed

In a large, heavy saucepan, combine above ingredients, and simmer slowly while you prepare the vegetables.

2 medium-sized zucchini, cut into 1/4-inch slices
2 large sweet red or green bell peppers, seeded, membranes removed, cut lengthwise into 1/2-inch slices
1 9-ounce package frozen artichoke hearts, thawed and drained
3 stalks celery cut into 1-inch pieces
1 cup sliced fresh mushroom caps

Add vegetables and mushrooms to sauce, cover, and simmer, stirring occasionally until they're tender but still crisp, 8 to 10 minutes. Remove from heat, uncover, and allow to cool; then cover and chill in refrigerator for several hours or overnight.

Lettuce
Sliced pitted mammoth ripe olives

Serve the salad on individual lettuce-lined plates, lifting the vegetables from the sauce with a slotted spoon, and topping each serving with a small amount of the sauce and a garnish of sliced ripe olives.

CABBAGE SALAD FIT FOR A KING

You probably more readily associate cabbages with kings than with pineapples and peanuts. As a consequence, we think you will be intrigued by the novelty of this salad and pleased by how good all of it tastes.

PREPARATION TIME 10 MINUTES   **SERVES 6 AS A SIDE DISH**

4   cups shredded red cabbage
1   cup crushed pineapple, drained
$^1/_2$ cup unsalted peanuts

Toss cabbage, pineapple, and peanuts together in a salad bowl.

$^1/_2$ cup light sour cream or plain low-fat yogurt
1   teaspoon honey
$^1/_4$ teaspoon celery seeds
     Freshly ground black pepper to taste

Combine sour cream or yogurt and seasonings and pour over cabbage mixture. Toss all together and refrigerate until served.

CURRIED COUSCOUS SALAD WITH CHICKPEAS

This quick and easy salad is a treat for the eyes as well as the palate. Top it off with a dollop of plain low-fat yogurt.

PREPARATION TIME 15 MINUTES   SERVES 4 TO 6

1¹/₂ cups water

Bring water to a boil.

1   cup couscous
¹/₂ cup raisins
¹/₂ teaspoon turmeric
1   tablespoon curry powder

Mix the above ingredients in a bowl and add the boiling water, stirring. Cover bowl with foil or a large plate and set aside at least 5 minutes.

2   cups cooked chickpeas or 1 16-ounce can chickpeas, rinsed and drained
¹/₂ cup sweet onion, diced
¹/₂ cup red bell pepper, diced

In a large bowl, mix the chickpeas, onions, and peppers.

2   tablespoon chopped fresh mint
3   tablespoon plain low-fat yogurt
¹/₄ teaspoon Tabasco sauce (more or less to taste)
     Freshly ground black pepper to taste

Add the couscous mixture to the chickpea mixture. Stir in the chopped mint, yogurt, tabasco, and pepper.

DILLED CARROTS

Salads that can be made ahead and kept in the refrigerator for several days are a real convenience. They're especially useful, when entertaining, for buffets.

PREPARATION TIME 15 MINUTES   SERVES 6 AS A SIDE DISH
CHILLING TIME 1 HOUR OR LONGER

> 8   large carrots
>   Boiling water

Peel carrots and cut into ¼-inch slices. Place in steamer basket over boiling water and steam until just tender, about 7 minutes. Plunge immediately into cold water. Drain well, and turn into a serving bowl.

> 1   medium-size mild onion, thinly sliced
> 2   tablespoons finely chopped fresh dill
> ⅔   cup French dressing, (see recipe that follows) made with
>   1 clove garlic, crushed

Separate the onion into rings and add to the carrots. Sprinkle with dill. Pour the dressing over the vegetables. Cover and chill. If chilled longer than 1 hour, remove from refrigerator 30 minutes before serving.

FRENCH DRESSING

PREPARATION TIME 5 MINUTES   MAKES ABOUT ¾ CUP

> 3   tablespoons wine vinegar or lemon juice, or a combination
> ½   cup extra-virgin olive oil
> ½   teaspoon dry mustard or 1 teaspoon prepared Dijon mustard
> ½   teaspoon salt
>   Freshly ground black pepper to taste

Place all ingredients in a small jar with a screw-top lid and shake vigorously. Or blend all together in a blender or food processor.

Note:
There are many delightful additions you can make to a simple French dressing. To name a few: a crushed clove of garlic, a little sesame paste (or a sprinkling of sesame seeds), herbs, parsley.

GAZPACHO SALAD

In an earlier chapter, we referred to one of our soups as "the 'pizza' you eat with a spoon." Well, here's a soup (gazpacho) you can eat with a fork! As mentioned earlier, agar (also known as *agar-agar* or *kanten*) is a tasteless jelling agent made from seaweed. It comes in bars, granules, flakes, or powder; the flakes are the easiest to come by and are available in most natural food stores. If you have agar in a form other than flakes, adjust the amount to use for jelling 4 cups of juice.

PREPARATION AND COOKING TIME 20 MINUTES   SERVES 6 TO 8
SETTING TIME ABOUT 2 HOURS

- 4   cups tomato juice
- 2   tablespoons agar powder (use a coffee grinder to turn the flakes to powder)
- 1   tablespoon chopped fresh basil or 1 teaspoon dried basil
- 2   tablespoons fresh lemon juice
- $1/2$ teaspoon Tabasco (or more to taste)

Bring tomato juice to a boil, sprinkle agar over the surface, and simmer, stirring with a wire whisk, for 5 minutes. Remove from heat and add the basil, lemon juice, and Tabasco.

- $1/2$ cup chopped celery
- $1/2$ cup chopped green bell pepper
- $1/2$ cup grated carrot

Stir all the vegetables into the tomato juice mixture. Rinse a 6-cup mold with cold water and pour in the gazpacho. Allow the mixture to cool to room temperature and then place it in the refrigerator until set.

- 2   medium cucumbers, peeled and sliced
    Nonfat plain yogurt or light sour cream
    Chopped fresh dill

To unmold salad, loosen around the edge with a knife, dip bottom of mold in hot water briefly, hold a serving dish over the top, and invert. The salad should drop out easily. If it does not, repeat dipping. Surround the salad ring with sliced cucumbers and serve with yogurt or sour cream and dill.

GREEK SALAD

Instead of preparation time, we thought it would be better to suggest the best procedure for assembling this salad with dispatch: (1) Clean all the vegetables to be used. (2) Slice them. (3) Arrange them. (4) Season them. Different dressings for different items provide pleasing surprises. When possible, use the dressings you have on hand.

Here's one Greek salad we prepared as a guide—also to be made and enjoyed—and to encourage you to try your hand at making your own variations.

SERVES 4

1	head Romaine, iceberg, or salad bowl lettuce (spinach may be substituted or used in addition)
1	medium onion, thinly sliced
8	mushrooms, cleaned and sliced
6	cherry tomatoes, halved
1	peeled cucumber, sliced
2	cups cooked chickpeas (garbanzo beans), or 1 can chickpeas, rinsed and drained

Arrange attractively on a large platter to suit your fancy.

$1/4$	cup vinegar, sweetened with sugar to taste
2	tablespoons fresh lemon juice
$1/2$	cup French Dressing (see page 89)
	Freshly ground pepper
	Feta cheese
	Cracked wheat bread, toasted

Put the sweetened vinegar on the cucumber slices, the lemon juice on the chickpeas and cherry tomato halves, and the French Dressing on the mushrooms. Add freshly ground pepper and crumbled feta cheese over everything. Serve with thick slices of toasted cracked wheat bread.

KASHA SALAD WITH BROCCOLI AND PEAS

This is an especially tasty salad with a crunch.

PREPARATION TIME 15 MINUTES
COOKING TIME ABOUT 17 MINUTES

| 1 | cup buckwheat kernels (kasha) |

Toast in a large skillet over medium heat for 5 minutes.

| 2 | cups boiling water |
| 2 | tablespoons unsalted butter |

Add butter and toasted kasha to the boiling water, cover, and cook on low heat for 10 to 12 minutes. Remove cover.

| 1 | cup broccoli florets |
| 1/2 | cup frozen peas |

While kasha is cooking, microwave the broccoli florets with 1 tablespoon of water on High for 1 1/2 minutes. Add peas and microwave 1 additional minute. Remove from microwave and allow to cool uncovered. Add broccoli and peas to the kasha.

1/4	cup toasted sunflower seeds
	Reduced-sodium soy sauce to taste
	Freshly ground black pepper to taste
	Red-leaf lettuce
1/2	cup sliced fennel

Add the seeds, soy sauce, and plenty of pepper to the kasha mixture. Serve on a bed of red-leaf lettuce surrounded by fennel.

LENTIL SALAD

This is a delicious main course salad, rich in protein. For the best flavor, the salad should stay overnight in the refrigerator.

PREPARATION TIME 15 MINUTES   SERVES 8
COOKING TIME 20 TO 40 MINUTES

- 2 cups washed lentils (or 4 cups hot, cooked lentils)
- 6 cups water
- 1 clove garlic, crushed
- $1/4$ teaspoon salt
- 3 tablespoons red wine vinegar
- $1/2$ teaspoon dry mustard
- $2/3$ cup extra-virgin olive oil
  Freshly ground pepper to taste
  Pinch ground cloves
  Dried herbs (tarragon or basil)

Cook lentils until as tender as you wish (20 to 40 minutes), drain, and keep warm. Mix garlic with the salt and mush thoroughly together with the back of a wooden spoon. Beat in the vinegar and dry mustard. Place mixture in a small glass jar with a screw top and add oil, a few grinds of pepper, cloves, and a pinch or two of herbs. Shake well to blend. Toss the lentils with the dressing.

- 2 small onions, thinly sliced
- 1 green bell pepper, seeded and diced

Add vegetables and toss again. Taste for seasoning. Refrigerate.

Suggestion:
Serve surrounded with quartered tomatoes and sprinkled with bits of chopped pimiento and chopped scallions. On the buffet table, Gazpacho Salad and Lentil Salad make a good team.

MIDDLE EASTERN BREAD SALAD

Instead of croutons in their salads, chefs in the Middle East often use split, toasted, and broken pita bread. This bread salad is a blend of garden-fresh vegetables seasoned in the Mediterranean style.

PREPARATION TIME 20 MINUTES   **SERVES 4 TO 6**

$^1/_2$ cup Lebanese Salad Dressing (see recipe below)
2   medium-sized tomatoes, diced
1   cucumber (peeled, if waxed), sliced
1   green bell pepper, seeded and cut into strips
4   green onions (scallions) chopped, including tops
1   carrot, peeled and shredded
6   radishes, sliced
1   small head lettuce (iceberg, romaine, escarole, etc.) or a mixture of several kinds, torn into bits

Pour the salad dressing into a large salad bowl. Add all the ingredients, ending with the lettuce. Do not toss. Cover bowl and refrigerate until serving time.

1   large pita bread

Just before serving, split and toast the pita and break it into pieces. Add bread to the salad bowl and toss, spooning dressing up through the salad.

LEBANESE SALAD DRESSING

The sage leaves make this typically Lebanese.

PREPARATION TIME 5 MINUTES   **MAKES $^2/_3$ CUP**

$^1/_3$ cup extra-virgin olive oil
$^1/_3$ cup lemon juice
1   clove garlic, crushed
$^1/_2$ teaspoon salt
     Freshly ground black pepper
4 or 5 fresh sage leaves, chopped

Combine all ingredients in a small jar with a screw-top lid. Shake well. If possible, allow to stand for a short time before using.

RICE SALAD MARBELLA

This splendid buffet salad is a Spanish classic. The rice mixture may be made as much as a day ahead, and it will only improve with waiting. Besides being stunning to look at, this salad is nourishing and refreshing.

PREPARATION TIME 20 MINUTES   SERVES 6 TO 8

3¹/₂ cups cooked brown rice
2   green bell peppers, chopped
1   small onion, chopped
2   cloves garlic, minced
³/₄ cup coarsely chopped almonds or walnuts
1   tablespoon chopped parsley

Combine ingredients in a large mixing bowl.

¹/₃ cup extra-virgin olive oil
3   tablespoons red wine vinegar
1   teaspoon paprika
¹/₂ teaspoon salt
¹/₄ teaspoon freshly ground black pepper

Put these ingredients in a small jar, cover, shake well to blend, and pour over the rice mixture. Toss until all ingredients are well mixed. Refrigerate until serving time.

    Lettuce
1   cup canned beans, any variety, drained and rinsed
3   medium tomatoes, quartered
2   tablespoons chopped fresh basil or parsley, or other fresh herb
    Salt and pepper to taste

On a large, shallow serving platter, arrange a bed of lettuce. Mound the rice mixture in the center, smoothing it with the back of a spoon. Surround the salad with a decorative arrangement of beans and tomato wedges. Sprinkle wedges lightly with salt and pepper and scatter chopped herbs over all.

TACO SALAD

Try Cold Cucumber-Mint Soup (see page 71) or Carrot Soup (see page 70) served cold with this hearty salad.

PREPARATION TIME 25 MINUTES   SERVES 6
COOKING TIME 15 MINUTES

Prepare the Spicy Taco Pita recipe (see page 64) up to and including folding in the almonds.

> Head of lettuce (your choice)
> Tortilla chips
> Grated Cheddar cheese
> Diced scallions, both green and white parts
> Fresh tomato wedges
> Avocado slices drenched in fresh lemon juice

Each serving should have a bed of lettuce with a big scoop of spicy taco salad in the center. Around the salad, put a layer of chips; then alternate tomato wedges and avocado slices. Sprinkle salad with grated cheese and diced scallions.

TOMATO, CUCUMBER, AND ARUGULA SALAD

Arugula, also known as *rocket* or *rugula*, is a spicy plant that can give a pleasantly peppery edge to a salad. Poppy Seed Dressing works well here, as does Watercress Dressing (see following page). Or try any extra-virgin olive oil and sweet balsamic vinegar dressing.

PREPARATION TIME 15 MINUTES   SERVES 4 AS A SIDE DISH

> 5 to 6 leaves romaine lettuce
> 5 to 6 leaves red- or green-leaf lettuce
> Handful of arugula leaves

Wash and dry lettuce and tear into salad bowl.

> 1   fresh ripe tomato, cut in small wedges
> 1/2 cucumber, thinly sliced
> 1/2 sweet onion, chopped coarsely
>   Fresh or dried dill to taste

Add vegetables on top of the greens and sprinkle with dill.

POPPY SEED DRESSING

This dressing makes a delicious complement to any leafy-green salad.

PREPARATION TIME 10 MINUTES   **MAKES 1 1/2 CUPS**

- 1/2 medium-sized sweet onion
- 1 cup extra-virgin olive oil
- 1/3 cup red wine vinegar
- 1 teaspoon dry mustard
- 2 tablespoons honey
    Dash of freshly ground pepper
- 1 tablespoon poppy seeds

In a food processor or blender, chop the onion. Add oil, vinegar, mustard, and honey and blend well. Pour dressing into container and stir in a dash of pepper, to taste, and the poppy seeds. Cover and refrigerate. Shake well before using.

WATERCRESS DRESSING

This speckled-green dressing is creamy and smooth with the watercress supplying a nice "bite."

PREPARATION TIME 5 MINUTES   **MAKES APPROXIMATELY 2 CUPS**

- 1 clove garlic, peeled
- 1/4 teaspoon salt
- 1 bunch watercress, washed and dried
- 1 cup low-fat mayonnaise (or more to taste)

With motor running, drop garlic into container of blender or food processor. Add salt. Divide watercress into 3 or 4 batches and add them one at a time. Blend until well chopped. Add mayonnaise and blend until just mixed.

TOMATO AND FETA SALAD

This quick and easy salad is a welcome addition to any buffet table, picnic, or Greek-style dinner.

PREPARATION TIME 15 MINUTES   **SERVES 6 AS A SIDE DISH**

- ¹/₄ cup minced parsley
- ¹/₄ cup minced sweet onion
- 1   clove garlic, minced
- 6   tablespoons fresh lemon juice
- 5   tablespoons extra-virgin olive oil
- ¹/₈ teaspoon cayenne

Mix the above ingredients well.

- 3 to 4 large fresh tomatoes, diced (about 2 cups)
- ¹/₂ cup feta cheese, crumbled
- Canned pitted ripe olives (optional)

Combine the tomatoes and feta cheese, pour dressing (reshake if necessary) over mixture, and stir lightly to coat. Garnish with pitted olives.

CUCUMBER AND APPLE SALAD

This sweet green salad is a welcome side dish on any plate.

PREPARATION TIME 10 MINUTES   **SERVES 4 AS A SIDE DISH**

- ¹/₂ head romaine lettuce
- 1   Granny Smith apple, peeled and sliced thin
- Fresh lemon juice
- 1   cucumber, peeled and thinly sliced
- 2   tablespoons coarsely chopped walnuts
- 2   tablespoons raisins
- 1¹/₂ tablespoons low-fat vanilla yogurt (more or less to taste)

Wash lettuce (discard outer leaves) and tear into bite-sized pieces in a salad bowl. Cover the apple slices with a splash of fresh lemon juice and add to the lettuce. Add cucumber, walnuts, and raisins. Mix in the vanilla yogurt to coat evenly.

PEAR AND PLUM SALAD

This might be called "Pear, Plum, and Other Nuances Salad," for it is a medley of sensory subtleties.

PREPARATION TIME 15 MINUTES   SERVES 6 AS A SIDE DISH

- 4 cups shredded green cabbage
- 6 ripe plums, cut into small chunks
- 1/2 cup low-fat mayonnaise
- 1/2 cup light sour cream
- 1/4 cup chopped walnuts
- 3 ripe Bartlett pears, cut into small chunks and coated with 2 tablespoons fresh lemon juice
- 1/4 teaspoon salt
- 2 tablespoons chopped crystallized ginger

Combine all ingredients, tossing thoroughly. Keep refrigerated until served.

PLATA DE FRUTAS

When we vacation in Mexico or the Caribbean, one of our favorite breakfasts is a large tray of fresh fruit: luscious familiar fruit, such as ripe slices of pineapple, mango, banana, and papaya, and others that are unfamiliar, exotic, and delicious. At home, we sometimes make up our own *platas de frutas*, using all the above along with kiwi, passion fruit, persimmon, fresh figs and whatever else is available.

Here's a tray salad that is ideal for a festive brunch or lunch, served with cottage cheese and warm, herb-flavored whole wheat rolls. Vary the selection of fruit according to what's around.

PREPARATION TIME 20 MINUTES   SERVES 8

3	large bananas, cut in 1-inch diagonal slices
2	medium-sized avocados, pitted, peeled, and sliced
	Lime juice
	Lettuce
1/2	medium-sized fresh pineapple, peeled, cored, and cubed, or 1 mango, peeled and sliced
2	California seedless oranges, peeled and sliced crosswise
1	cup seedless grapes, halved
3	tablespoons chopped crystallized ginger

Dip the bananas and avocados in the lime juice to prevent darkening. On a large lettuce-lined tray, arrange the various fruits, keeping each variety separate. Sprinkle the chopped ginger over the top and cover with plastic wrap. Refrigerate until serving time.

1/4   cup chopped cashew nuts or almonds

Scatter nuts over the top. Serve Lime Dressing (which follows) separately.

LIME DRESSING

PREPARATION TIME 5 MINUTES   MAKES 1 CUP

- 1/3   cup lime juice
- 1/2   cup canola oil
- 2   tablespoons dark rum
- 1   tablespoon honey
- 1/2   teaspoon ground coriander

Mix all ingredients together. If refrigerated, bring to room temperature and stir well before using.

SPINACH AND STRAWBERRY SALAD

Strawberries are a wonderful addition to a tossed green salad. They're often overlooked, and they're usually available year-round. This salad is a good accompaniment to Kasha and Chickpeas (see page 156) served with corn on the cob.

PREPARATION TIME 10 MINUTES   SERVES 6 TO 8 AS A SIDE DISH

- 8 to 10 ounces fresh spinach
- 3/4 to 1 cup sliced fresh strawberries
- 1/4   cup slivered almonds (optional garnish)

Wash, dry, and chop spinach. Place into salad bowl and toss in the sliced strawberries. Try the Poppy Seed Dressing (page 97), Out-of-Sight Dressing (page 102), or any simple vinaigrette on this salad. Garnish with almonds if desired.

OUT-OF-SIGHT DRESSING

It's out of sight because it goes in the bottom of the bowl with the salad on top until tossed. Especially recommended for a tossed green salad of different kinds of lettuce and raw spinach.

PREPARATION TIME 5 MINUTES   **MAKES APPROXIMATELY ⅓ CUP**

> Small clove garlic
> ¼ teaspoon salt

Dice garlic into salad bowl. Scatter salt over garlic; then mash the salted garlic with the back of a teaspoon.

> ¼ cup extra-virgin olive oil
> 2 tablespoons balsamic vinegar

Pour into the salad bowl. Stir to combine all ingredients. Refrigerate while salad is being made. Place salad over dressing and refrigerate. When you're ready to serve, toss the salad so that all of it is coated with dressing.

Breads

These days, there are many good breads to be found at the bakery, deli, and supermarket, so why bake your own?

- Do it for the pleasure involved and for the discovery of what this ancient skill involves. It isn't difficult. It actually can be quick and easy, as our recipes show.
- Perhaps on closer inspection of the breads available in your market, you may find that labels of "whole wheat" and "multigrain" aren't all they purport to be.
- Perhaps you live in an area where only squishy-soft breads are available.
- Perhaps you'd like the pleasure of discovering new breads not commonly available in stores.

All are good reasons to exercise your talents as a bread baker and to learn and enjoy the rewards of being in control of what goes into your staff of life.

CHAPATTI—A CIRCULAR DELIGHT

If you need bread and are pressed for time, try chapatti, a flat bread from northern India with a delicious whole-grain flavor. Chapattis are as nourishing as they are simple. Use them as you would any bread.

PREPARATION TIME 15 MINUTES
COOKING TIME 12 TO 18 MINUTES

MAKES 6 TO 8 CHAPATTI

- $^1/_2$ cup yellow cornmeal
- 1 cup whole wheat flour
- $^1/_8$ teaspoon salt

Mix together thoroughly.

- 2 tablespoons soft, unsalted butter

Cut the butter into the flour-cornmeal mixture. (This can be done most easily in a food processor, using the cutting blade.)

- $^1/_2$ cup cold water (approximately)

Add only enough water to make the ingredients cling together in a ball. Cut this ball into 6 to 8 pieces. Flatten each piece on a floured board with the palm of the hand and then roll with a rolling pin until each piece is 5 to 6 inches in diameter. To make the pieces circular, keep turning them over between rolls of the rolling pin. Cook on a hot, buttered griddle until brown areas appear, 3 to 4 minutes on each side.

Note: Other flour, bran, and cornmeal combinations: (1) 1 cup whole wheat flour, $^1/_2$ cup bran. (2) 1 cup cornmeal, $^1/_4$ cup bran, $^1/_4$ cup whole wheat flour. (3) 1 cup cornmeal, $^1/_2$ cup whole wheat flour. Experiment with other combinations. You might also try using low-fat milk instead of water.

COFFEE CAN BREAD

This bread requires no kneading and only one rising; it has a light, fine texture and a tantalizing aroma of ginger and herbs. You make it in 1-pound coffee cans equipped with plastic lids.

PREPARATION TIME 30 MINUTES   MAKES 2 LOAVES
RISING TIME 35 TO 45 MINUTES
BAKING TIME 45 TO 55 MINUTES
Near end of rising time, preheat oven to 350°.

1¹/₃ packages (4 teaspoons) active dry yeast
¹/₂   cup warm water
      Pinch of sugar

In a large mixing bowl, sprinkle yeast over warm water, add sugar, and stir to dissolve yeast. Place bowl in a warm spot until mixture foams, about 15 minutes.

1¹/₂ cups low-fat milk
¹/₄   cup (¹/₂ stick) unsalted butter cut in 4 pieces
3   tablespoons honey
1   teaspoon grated fresh ginger or ¹/₄ teaspoon ground ginger
1   teaspoon chopped fresh dill or ¹/₄ teaspoon dried dillweed
¹/₄   teaspoon dried basil
¹/₄   teaspoon dried oregano
¹/₄   teaspoon dried thyme
1   teaspoon salt

While yeast is standing, scald milk and stir in remaining ingredients. Cool mixture to lukewarm. Pour into the yeast and mix well.

1¹/₂ cups whole wheat flour
3   cups unbleached, all-purpose flour (approximately)

Beat flour into the liquid ingredients, 1 cup at a time, beating very well after each addition. (Use an electric mixer if possible.) Use all the whole wheat flour first; then add the white until batter forms a dough that will hold together in a ball but is too sticky to knead. Divide dough in half and pack each half into a well-greased 1-pound coffee can. Press dough down firmly with greased knuckles to make sure there are no air pockets. Cover with well-greased plastic lids. (At this point, dough may be frozen for several weeks.)

Set cans in a warm spot until the dough rises and bursts out of the tops of the cans, carrying the lids with it. *Near end of rising time, preheat oven at 350°.* (Frozen dough should be allowed to stand at room temperature until the lid pops off, usually 4 or 5 hours.) Remove lids if they are still clinging to the tops of the dough, and bake the loaves in the preheated oven until puffy crown is well browned, 45 to 55 minutes. Loosen crust around top edges with a thin knife and slide loaves from the cans. Cool them on a rack in upright position.

CRACKED WHEAT FRENCH BREAD

To the delightful crisp crust of French bread, we've added the crunch of cracked wheat.

PREPARATION TIME 30 MINUTES   MAKES 2 LONG LOAVES
RISING TIME 20 MINUTES
BAKING TIME 40 MINUTES

> 1¹/₄ cups cracked wheat (bulgur)
> 1 tablespoon salt (or less)
> 1¹/₂ cups boiling water

Put cracked wheat in a large mixing bowl, add salt, pour in boiling water, and mix. Cool to lukewarm (110° to 115°). You can speed this up by putting the mixing bowl in a larger bowl containing cold water.

> 1 tablespoon brown sugar
> ³/₄ cup lukewarm water
> 1 package (1 tablespoon) active dry yeast

Put sugar in water and stir. Add yeast and stir again. When yeast has bubbled up and become foamy (in 5 to 10 minutes) and cracked wheat mixture has cooled to lukewarm, add the yeast and its water into the cracked wheat mixture.

> 1¹/₂ cups whole wheat flour
> 3 cups unbleached, all-purpose flour

Add the flours to the mixture, knead, and make a soft dough. (Use more flour if needed.) Put the dough in a greased bowl, revolve dough to grease it. Cover. Turn the oven to warm (150°). After 1¹/₂ minutes, turn off the oven. Put the bowl in the turned-off oven for 15 minutes.

Take dough from oven and punch it down. Divide the dough into two equal pieces. Shape each piece into a long French loaf by rolling the dough on a board and/or between your hands.

Sprinkle cornmeal on two ungreased cookie sheets. Put the loaves on the cookie sheets and let them rise for 5 minutes.

With a sharp knife, makes 3 or 4 diagonal slashes, ¹/₈-inch deep, in each loaf. Brush the loaves with cold water. Place them in the oven and turn the heat to 400°. Put a container of boiling water under the loaves. Bake 40 minutes.

Should any of the bread be left after a day or two, it makes fine toast.

ONE-RISE ANADAMA

A subtle blend of corn and wheat flours. You'll also find the salted crust a delicious, intriguing contrast.

PREPARATION TIME 20 MINUTES

MAKES 3 LOAVES

RISING TIME 30 MINUTES

BAKING TIME 30 TO 40 MINUTES

Near end of rising time, preheat oven to 350°.

$1/2$ cup cold water
$1/2$ cup yellow cornmeal
$1^1/2$ cups boiling water
$1/2$ cup molasses
2   tablespoons canola oil

Mix cornmeal in cold water and then add boiling water, molasses, and oil. Cool to lukewarm (110°).

$1/2$ cup lukewarm water
2   tablespoons active dry yeast
1   tablespoon sugar

Combine and set aside until ingredients become very foamy.

3   tablespoons gluten ($1^1/2$ teaspoons per cup of flour)
1   teaspoon salt
$1/4$ cup granular lecithin (optional)
6   cups unbleached all-purpose flour (approximately)

Put all the ingredients in electric mixer bowl *except* for 1 cup or so of the flour.

$3^3/4$ cups hot water (120°F)

Pour water slowly into bowl while paddle mixes. When water is used up, add extra flour as needed to make a fairly stiff dough. Change paddle for dough hook when mix thickens. Shape dough into 3 loaves for pans sized $8^1/2$ by $4^1/4$ by $2^3/4$ inches. Place loaves, covered with towels, in a barely warmed, then turned off oven. In 30 minutes or so, the loaves should become big and well shaped.

1   tablespoon cornmeal
$1/2$ teaspoon salt
      Canola oil or melted unsalted butter

Mix cornmeal and salt. Brush tops of loaves with oil or butter. Sift cornmeal mixture over bread. Bake in 350° oven for 30 to 40 minutes.

Note: Gluten is available in health food stores.

SIXTY-MINUTES ROLLS

These dinner rolls can be made and baked in just 60 minutes. They are delicious while still oven-hot, when cooled a bit, or even cold.

PREPARATION TIME 18 MINUTES   MAKES 24 ROLLS
RISING TIME 30 MINUTES
BAKING TIME 12 MINUTES
After dough has risen, preheat oven to 425°.

2³/₄	cups unbleached, all-purpose flour
³/₄	cup whole wheat flour
3	tablespoons sugar
2	packages (2 tablespoons) active dry yeast
1	teaspoon salt

Mix dry ingredients together thoroughly.

1	cup low-fat milk
¹/₂	cup water
¹/₄	cup unsalted butter

Heat liquids and butter in a saucepan over low heat. Butter does not need to melt but liquid should be very warm (120° to 130°). If you don't have a thermometer, test the liquid on your wrist; liquid should feel a bit more than warm but not hot. Gradually add liquid to flour mixture and beat in an electric mixer or with a spoon.

1¹/₂ cups unbleached all-purpose flour (approximately)

Add flour until dough is no longer sticky; use more if necessary. Knead until dough has an elastic quality. Place dough in greased bowl. Turn until bottom is greased; then turn so greased side is up. Cover, place bowl in a pan of lukewarm water, and let dough rise for 15 minutes. Punch dough down. On a floured board, divide dough into 2 or 3 parts, depending on the number of shapes you are going to make. The simplest shape is a ball, made by rolling a small piece of dough between the palms of the hands. Three 1-inch diameter balls, dipped in butter and placed in a muffin tin, will produce a cloverleaf roll. Or you can fashion pan rolls simply by making 2-inch balls, dipping them in butter, and placing them in a layer cake pan so that they touch each other. Or a 2-inch ball can be transformed into a dinner roll. With floured hands, roll the ball between the hands until it is 4 inches long and taper its ends. Bake these rolls 1 inch apart on greased cookie sheets.

Cover shaped rolls and let them rise in warm oven (90°) for 15 minutes.

Preheat oven to 425°. Bake rolls for 12 minutes. Remove from baking sheets and cool on wire racks.

APPLE-CORIANDER MUFFINS

In making muffins, the liquid ingredients should be mixed into the dry until just barely combined, about 10 or 12 stirs.

PREPARATION TIME 15 MINUTES
BAKING TIME 25 MINUTES
Preheat oven to 375°.

MAKES 12 MUFFINS

- ¹/₄ cup unsalted butter
- 6 tablespoons brown sugar (firmly packed)
- 1 large egg
- ¹/₂ cup milk
- ¹/₂ cup coarsely grated, peeled apple

Cream butter and sugar together until well mixed and fluffy. Beat in egg and milk and blend well. Stir in apple.

- 1¹/₄ cups unbleached, all-purpose flour
- 3 tablespoons wheat germ
- 2 teaspoons baking powder
- ¹/₄ teaspoon ground coriander
- 1 teaspoon cinnamon
- ¹/₂ cup chopped walnuts

Blend dry ingredients together in a large mixing bowl, stirring in walnuts last. Make a well in the center and pour wet ingredients into it all at once. Stir just until dry mixture is no longer visible. Spray muffin pans with oil. Spoon batter into tins, filling cups ²/₃ full. Bake until lightly browned, about 25 minutes. Remove at once from tins and serve. If muffins are allowed to cool, reheat them in a tightly closed paper bag at 350° for about 5 minutes.

BRAN MUFFINS

This bran muffin batter keeps in the refrigerator for several weeks.

3 cups unprocessed bran
1 cup boiling water

Mix bran and water. Cool.

2 large eggs or egg substitute
2 cups buttermilk
1/2 cup canola oil
1 cup raisins

Add the above ingredients to the bran-water mixture and combine thoroughly.

2 1/2 teaspoons baking soda
1/2 teaspoon salt
2/3 cup sugar
2 1/2 cups whole wheat flour

Blend these dry ingredients; then stir into the liquid mixture. The batter may be used immediately or kept in the refrigerator for future use. Before using, stir batter to distribute raisins. Spray muffin tins with oil and fill 3/4 full. Bake for 20 minutes.

Optional: Sprinkle each muffin with chopped walnuts before baking.

BANANA MILKSHAKE MUFFINS

Mix the dry ingredients for these muffins the night before and you can have them quickly in the morning, fresh and hot, by blending and adding the fruit and liquids, and baking.

PREPARATION TIME 15 MINUTES   MAKES 12 MUFFINS
BAKING TIME 25 MINUTES
Preheat oven to 400°.

2	cups unbleached, all-purpose flour
1/2	cup white sugar
1/2	cup wheat germ
2	tablespoons baking powder
1/2	cup chopped nuts (walnuts, peanuts, almonds)
1/4	cup currants (or chopped dry apricots)
1	teaspoon cinnamon

Mix these ingredients together. This can be done the night before. Spray a 12-muffin baking pan lightly with oil.

1	large egg
1	cup skim milk or buttermilk
3	tablespoons canola oil
1	large banana, cut in pieces

Mix in blender. Add to dry ingredients and, with a tablespoon, mix just enough for a uniform batter. Distribute batter in the 12 cups of the baking tin. Bake for 25 minutes. Turn muffins out onto a cooling rack. They are ready to eat.

BOB'S BANANA MUFFINS

These muffins are similar to the Banana Milkshake Muffins in that they are quick and easy to make and delicious to eat. They differ, however, in that they contain no dairy products.

PREPARATION TIME 15 MINUTES   MAKES 12 MUFFINS
BAKING TIME 15 TO 20 MINUTES
Preheat oven to 375°.

1¹/₂ cups whole wheat pastry flour
¹/₂ teaspoon baking soda
1¹/₂ teaspoons baking powder
1 teaspoon cinnamon
¹/₄ teaspoon freshly grated nutmeg

Sift ingredients together. Spray a standard 12-muffin baking pan lightly with oil.

3 tablespoons canola oil
¹/₂ cup dark molasses
1 cup mashed banana (about 2 large bananas)
¹/₂ cup raisins

Mix these ingredients together. Add to dry ingredients and mix just enough to blend. Pour batter into the muffin tins and bake for 15 to 20 minutes. Empty muffins onto a rack to cool.

CORNBREAD

Technically, a quick bread is one that uses a leavening agent other than yeast. Since this one uses baking powder, it is officially a quick bread.

PREPARATION TIME 15 MINUTES   MAKES 12 TO 16 SQUARES

BAKING TIME 30 MINUTES

Preheat oven to 400°.

1	cup unbleached, all-purpose flour
1/4	cup whole wheat flour
1/4	cup wheat germ
1 1/2	cups yellow cornmeal
1	tablespoon baking powder
1/8	teaspoon salt

Mix these dry ingredients thoroughly and set aside.

1/2	cup brown sugar (not packed)
1/2	cup canola oil
2	large eggs or egg substitute

Blend sugar and oil in electric mixer. Add eggs one at a time and blend them with the sugar and oil mixture.

1	cup low-fat milk

Alternate stirring a little of the milk and a little of the dry ingredients into the sugar, oil, and egg mixture. Pour the batter into an oiled and floured 8-inch square pan. Bake for 30 minutes. Cool in pan. Cut into squares and cool further on a rack.

FRUIT-NUT MUFFINS

The fruit and nuts in this recipe can be varied to suit whatever you may have on hand. If you bake these muffins regularly, changing the fruit and nuts used provides a welcome variety. Here is one of our most popular versions.

PREPARATION TIME 15 MINUTES   MAKES 12 MUFFINS
BAKING TIME 25 MINUTES
Preheat oven to 400°.

2	cups unbleached, all-purpose flour
¹/₂	cup white sugar
2	tablespoons baking powder
¹/₂	teaspoon cinnamon
¹/₂	cup wheat germ
¹/₂	cup chopped dried apricots
¹/₂	cup chopped cashews
1	Granny Smith apple, peeled, cored, chopped

In a large bowl, mix above ingredients.

1	large egg
3	tablespoons canola oil
1	cup skim or low-fat milk or buttermilk

In a small bowl, beat egg slightly, add oil, beat more, add milk, and stir. Add these liquid ingredients to previously mixed dry ingredients and mix together only until uniform. Spray a 12-cup muffin tin with oil; spoon batter equally into all cups. Bake for 25 minutes. Empty baked muffins onto rack to cool. In just a minute they're ready to enjoy.

NUT-RAISIN BREAD

This quick bread is as sweet as a dessert. And its deliciousness is enhanced by walnuts.

PREPARATION TIME 25 MINUTES   MAKES 2 LOAVES
BAKING TIME 45 MINUTES
Preheat oven to 350°.

$1/2$ cup canola oil
$1/2$ cup brown sugar (not packed)

Mix shortening and sugar until creamy in texture.

2 large eggs or egg substitute
1 cup low-fat milk

Add to creamed mixture and set aside.

3 cups whole wheat flour
4 teaspoons baking powder
$1/2$ teaspoon salt
1 cup coarsely chopped walnuts
1 cup raisins

Mix these dry ingredients thoroughly and combine with reserved mixture. Spoon equal amounts into two buttered $8^1/2$ by $4^1/2$-inch pans. (For a higher loaf, use a smaller pan, $7^1/4$ by $3^1/2$ inches.) Smooth surface with a spatula. Bake for 45 minutes. Remove from pans and cool on rack.

PUMPKIN MUFFINS

These muffins, a healthy treat for Halloween, can be enjoyed all year long thanks to the convenience of canned pumpkin. As with the Banana Milkshake Muffins, the dry ingredients can be mixed together the night before, enabling you to complete them quickly in the morning.

PREPARATION TIME 15 MINUTES   MAKES 12 MUFFINS
BAKING TIME 25 MINUTES
Preheat oven to 400°.

1¹/₂	cups unbleached, all-purpose flour
¹/₂	cup wheat germ
¹/₂	cup brown sugar
1	tablespoon baking powder
¹/₂	teaspoon baking soda
¹/₂	cup chopped walnuts
¹/₂	cup raisins
2	teaspoons cinnamon
¹/₂	teaspoon ground ginger
¹/₂	teaspoon freshly grated nutmeg
¹/₈	teaspoon ground cloves

Mix these ingredients together. Spray a 12-muffin baking pan lightly with oil.

1	large egg
¹/₂	cup buttermilk
1	cup canned pumpkin
3	tablespoons canola oil

Mix well in bowl or blender. Add to the dry ingredients, stirring just enough to blend. Pour batter evenly into muffin tins and bake for 15 to 20 minutes. Empty muffins onto a cooling rack.

SOY MUFFINS

A muffin that manages to be both nourishing and delicious. It can also be made in 1-2-3 fashion: (1) Assemble dry ingredients. (2) Assemble liquid ingredients. (3) Combine dry and liquid ingredients.

PREPARATION TIME 15 MINUTES
BAKING TIME 12 MINUTES
Preheat oven to 425°.

MAKES 12 MUFFINS

¹/₂	cup sifted soy flour
1	cup whole wheat flour
¹/₄	cup unbleached, all-purpose flour
¹/₄	cup wheat germ
1	tablespoon baking powder
1	teaspoon salt
¹/₄	cup sunflower seeds
¹/₂	cup raisins

Combine thoroughly, using an electric mixer if possible.

1	large egg
3	tablespoons oil
2	tablespoons honey
1	cup low-fat milk

Beat the egg with the oil, honey, and milk. Stir this mixture into the dry ingredients only enough to moisten them. Spoon into oiled muffin tins. Bake for 12 minutes. Cool muffins on a rack.

SUNFLOWER DINNER MUFFINS

Because of their sweet nature, muffins usually wind up on the breakfast or tea table. Nonsweet muffins, though, can fit in nicely at dinner. They're especially good with hearty soups.

PREPARATION TIME 15 MINUTES   MAKES 12 MUFFINS
BAKING TIME 25 MINUTES
Preheat oven to 375°.

> 1   large egg
> ¹/₄ cup canola oil
> ¹/₄ cup brown sugar (firmly packed)
> 1   cup low-fat milk

Beat ingredients together in a bowl until well mixed.

> 1   cup sifted unbleached all-purpose flour
> 1   cup unsifted whole wheat flour
> 1   tablespoon baking powder
> ¹/₂ teaspoon salt
> ¹/₂ cup sunflower seeds

Combine these dry ingredients in a large mixing bowl and make a well in the center. Pour egg mixture into the well and stir gently until ingredients are just moistened. Fill well-greased 2¹/₂-inch muffin cups ²/₃ full with batter. Bake for about 25 minutes, or until tops are rounded and lightly browned. Serve at once.

2>22>222

WHOLE WHEAT APRICOT SCONES

These whole wheat apricot scones are a delicious variation on the traditional scone. Serve warm with your favorite jam, cold, or slightly toasted.

PREPARATION TIME 20 MINUTES　　　　　　　　　　**MAKES 12 SCONES**
BAKING TIME 15 TO 20 MINUTES
Preheat oven to 400°.

- 1 cup low-fat plain yogurt
- 1 large egg
- 2 tablespoons sugar

Beat egg. Add yogurt and sugar.

- 3¼ cups whole wheat pastry flour
- 2 teaspoons baking powder
- 1 teaspoon baking soda
- ½ teaspoon salt

Sift the above ingredients and add to the egg mixture. Mix well.

- 3 tablespoons melted unsalted butter or canola oil
- ½ cup chopped dried apricots or prunes

Add butter and apricots and knead dough on a lightly floured surface for a couple minutes, adding more flour to form a stiff dough. Knead also to mix apricots evenly through dough. Cut dough into 3 pieces and pat each piece into a circle about 4 inches across. With a sharp knife, cut the circles into quarters. Place the scones on a buttered cookie sheet and bake for 15 to 20 minutes.

WHOLE WHEAT AND WALNUT BREAD

You could almost live on bread and water if this was your bread choice, though we don't know about the water.

PREPARATION TIME 20 MINUTES   **MAKES 2 LARGE LOAVES**
BAKING TIME 40 MINUTES
Preheat oven to 350°.

3	cups cold water
1/3	cup canola oil
1/3	cup honey
1	tablespoon salt

Warm water in microwave for 1 minute, but it should be no warmer than body temperature. Put it in mixer bowl; use batter beater. Add oil, honey, salt, and start mixer at low speed.

4	cups whole wheat flour
1/2	cup chopped walnuts
1	tablespoon dry yeast powder

At slow speed, gradually add flour. When it has thoroughly mixed with the liquid, add walnuts, then yeast and blend in well.

3	cups whole wheat flour
	Unsalted butter

Replace batter beater with dough hook, turn mixer to higher speed, and add the 3 cups of flour, continuing to knead for 5 to 7 minutes. During this time, butter two 9-by-5-inch bread pans and dust a little flour on the counter or board on which you'll be working. After 5 minutes or so, dough should feel slightly sticky. If it is stickier than that, add more flour, a little at a time. Remove dough and place on floured working surface, rolling it into a cylinder. Cut the dough into 2 equal parts. Roll each into a cylinder that will fit into the pans. Don't worry about the exact fit. It will all even up in the baking. Cover pans with a cloth and put them in a warm place to allow the dough to rise. This usually takes 30 to 40 minutes. The dough should increase so that its top is approximately even with the top of the pan. Now put the loaves in the oven to bake for 40 minutes. Remove pans from the oven, turn the loaves out onto a rack where they can cool. That's it!

WHOLE WHEAT BISCUITS

These hot and crunchy biscuits can brighten breakfast, lunch, or dinner.

PREPARATION TIME 10 MINUTES   MAKES 10 TO 13 BISCUITS
BAKING TIME ABOUT 15 MINUTES
Preheat oven to 400°.

    2   cups whole wheat flour
    4   teaspoons baking powder
    1   teaspoon salt
    ¹/₂   cup instant dry milk

Mix ingredients together thoroughly in the bowl of an electric mixer.

    ¹/₃   cup canola oil
    ²/₃   cup water

Combine oil and water and pour into dry ingredients. Stir just enough to moisten them. On a lightly floured board, knead dough briefly, merely folding it over a few times. Press the dough with your hands to a uniform ¹/₂-inch thickness. With a biscuit cutter or a glass with a diameter of 2¹/₂ inches, cut the dough into circles. Place them on an ungreased cookie sheet and bake for about 15 minutes until they're light brown.

Main Dishes

To the average person, dinner means a main dish of meat, poultry, or fish. All the rest is the supporting cast. A vegetable is something lightly dismissed.

In vegetarian cuisine, vegetables are the stars. One vegetable may occupy center stage, but more commonly two or three will play complementary roles, each balanced against the others for taste, texture, color, and nutrition. Many of the recipes here aren't even primarily vegetable. There are legumes, grains, fruits, seeds, nuts, and things like tofu and textured vegetable protein wedded to the vegetables. Breads, pastas, roots, and even flowers also become part of the picture. Herbs, spices, vinegars, and soy-derived sauces are playing an emerging role in creating an awareness of the superb range of tantalizing flavors and aromas that many people seldom encounter. The Japanese call it *awahrii*. It is a new awareness of what the eating experience can be.

ALMOND-SPINACH ROULADE

When you need a dish that's special—beautiful, different, and delicious—here's your answer. This roulade is especially good for entertaining because it can be prepared in advance and refrigerated; then it needs only a short crisping in melted butter just before serving.

PREPARATION TIME 20 MINUTES   SERVES 6
BAKING AND CRISPING TIME 30 MINUTES
Preheat oven to 375°.

    1   10-ounce package frozen spinach
    2   tablespoons unsalted butter

Remove spinach from package, allow to thaw, and drain well. Spray a 10-by-15-inch jelly roll pan with oil and set in the 375° oven for a few minutes to warm.

    2   cups skim milk
    1   large egg
    2   egg whites
    1   cup unbleached all-purpose flour
    1   teaspoon baking powder
    ¹/₂ teaspoon salt

Blend these ingredients in a food processor, blender, or electric mixer. Pour batter into pan, spreading evenly over the bottom. Bake for 20 to 25 minutes, or until it just barely starts to brown.

    2   tablespoons unsalted butter
    ³/₄ cup chopped, slivered, or sliced almonds
    ¹/₂ teaspoon dried thyme
    ¹/₈ teaspoon freshly grated nutmeg

While the oven pancake bakes, melt butter in a large skillet. Add almonds and sauté until lightly toasted, stirring frequently. Add thawed, drained spinach, thyme, and nutmeg and stir to mix.

When the oven pancake is baked, loosen it gently around the edges with a spatula and invert it, with a long edge facing you, on a clean dish towel. Spoon the spinach mixture evenly over it, spreading to all edges.

    2   cups grated mild Cheddar or Jack cheese

Sprinkle cheese over spinach and, using towel as an aid, start with the long edge and roll pancake up like a jelly roll. (If you wish to serve the roulade later, wrap it in foil and refrigerate.)

2   tablespoons unsalted butter

Melt butter in large skillet. Cut roll into 6 portions. Sauté portions slowly over moderately low heat, until browned and crisp outside and heated through.

Low-fat sour cream
Dijon mustard

Serve with sour cream to which you have added mustard to taste.

BARLEY, CHICKPEAS, AND WALNUTS

Barley was one of the first grains ever cultivated. Though it is a popular ingredient of soups, it seldom plays a leading role at dinner. But in this recipe, you'll agree it deserves top billing.

PREPARATION TIME 20 MINUTES   **SERVES 3 TO 4**
COOKING TIME 60 MINUTES

1   cup pearl barley
1¹/₂ tablespoons extra-virgin olive oil
2   cups vegetable broth

Wash barley until water runs clear; drain. In 12-inch pan heat barley until it is completely dry; then add oil. Continue toasting barley for 10 minutes, stirring occasionally. Transfer to 2-quart pot, and add broth. Cook at low heat, covered, for 45 minutes.

¹/₂ cup thinly sliced carrots
¹/₂ cup sliced green onions
¹/₂ teaspoon dried thyme
     Salt and pepper to taste
1   15 or 16 ounce can chickpeas, rinsed and drained

Add carrots, onions, and seasonings and cook for an additional 15 minutes, or until all liquid has been absorbed and barley is soft. In last 5 minutes, add chickpeas.

¹/₂ cup coarsely chopped walnuts, pan toasted

Sprinkle a few walnuts atop each serving. A green vegetable or salad is a good accompaniment.

BEAN AND CHEESE PATTIES

These eggless patties are broiled, not fried, and can be made with almost any variety of canned beans or cooked dry beans.

PREPARATION TIME 10 MINUTES   MAKES 8 TO 10 PATTIES
BAKING AND BROILING TIME 16 MINUTES

- 1¹/₂ cups canned or cooked dry beans
- ²/₃ cup sunflower seeds
- 3 tablespoons unsalted butter or margarine
- ¹/₄ cup ready-made spaghetti sauce
- ¹/₂ cup chopped onion

Blend all ingredients to a paste consistency in a blender or food processor. Put in mixing bowl.

- ¹/₂ cup canned or cooked dry beans
- ¹/₂ teaspoon chili powder
- 1 tablespoon reduced-sodium soy sauce
- 1 stalk celery, chopped
- 1 tablespoon wheat germ

Add these ingredients to the bowl, mix thoroughly, and shape into patties. If patties aren't firm, add more wheat germ. Put patties on a cookie sheet lightly sprayed with oil and bake for 10 minutes. Then broil for a few minutes until brown.

Sliced Cheddar cheese

Turn patties. Place a slice of cheese on the unbroiled sides. Broil until cheese melts.

BEANS, ITALIAN STYLE

You have your choice. You can prepare this recipe in a skillet on your stove top or in the oven in a casserole.

PREPARATION TIME 7 MINUTES   SERVES 4
COOKING TIME 10 MINUTES

   1   cup elbow macaroni

Cook according to package directions.

   1   medium onion, chopped
   1   stalk celery, chopped
   1   tablespoon minced parsley
   1   tablespoon chopped fresh basil or 1 teaspoon dried basil
   2   tablespoons extra-virgin olive oil

Sauté vegetables for 5 minutes.

   1   cup chopped cabbage
       Salt and pepper to taste

Stir cabbage and seasonings into sautéed vegetables. Cook cabbage a few minutes, until tender.

   1   15 to 16 ounce can kidney or pea beans, rinsed and drained
   1   cup plum tomatoes, drained and chopped

Add cooked macaroni, beans, and tomatoes to the cooking vegetables; bring to a simmer.

  ¼   cup freshly grated Parmesan cheese (or more to taste)
       Paprika

Remove skillet from heat, stir in cheese, and sprinkle with paprika. Serve.

Variation: Spoon macaroni and vegetables from skillet into a casserole, top with cheese, and sprinkle with paprika. Set under broiler until cheese melts and browns.

BEAN AND MUSHROOM STEW

You can use almost any kind of canned or cooked dry beans and almost any kind of edible mushroom in this recipe. Our preferred mushroom is shiitake.

PREPARATION TIME 7 MINUTES   SERVES 4
COOKING TIME 20 MINUTES

3   cups canned beans, rinsed and drained
2   cups vegetable broth
1   6-ounce can tomato paste
1   medium onion, chopped
1 or 2 cloves garlic, minced
1   cup sliced mushrooms
1   zucchini, about 6 inches long, thinly sliced
1   stalk celery, chopped
     Salt and pepper to taste
     Pinch each of cinnamon, allspice, cloves, nutmeg
¼ to ½ cup grated Cheddar cheese

Mix all ingredients in a 2-quart saucepan and simmer until vegetables are cooked. If stew is too thin, add wheat germ; if too thick, add water. Transfer to a serving dish, sprinkle with cheese, and serve.

BEANS WITH SPICES

Although there are numerous ingredients in this entrée, especially if one counts the condiments accompanying it, it can be produced quickly. The spices are a matter of individual taste. You can even settle for just curry powder, in which case use twice the amount specified.

PREPARATION TIME 10 MINUTES   SERVES 2 TO 3
COOKING TIME 10 MINUTES

$^1/_2$ teaspoon turmeric
$1^1/_2$ teaspoons ground cumin
$1^1/_2$ teaspoons curry powder
$^1/_2$ teaspoon cinnamon

Mix the spices together.

2   tablespoons unsalted butter or margarine

Melt the butter or margarine in a large skillet. Stir in the spices and cook for 1 minute.

$^1/_2$ cup chopped celery
$^1/_2$ cup chopped onion
2   medium carrots, thinly sliced
1   tablespoon cornstarch
1   cup cooked or canned beans, any variety
$^3/_4$ cup water or vegetable broth
4   ounces water chestnuts (optional)

Stir vegetables and other ingredients into the cooking spices. Simmer, covered, for 5 to 10 minutes, until vegetables are tender. Serve with salted peanuts, sliced green bell pepper, scallions, raisins, chopped hard-cooked eggs, or whatever else strikes your fancy.

BLACK BEANS AND RICE

Thick, dark, and spicy, this is a quick, meatless version of a festive South American dish called *feijoada*.

PREPARATION TIME 10 MINUTES   SERVES 4
COOKING TIME 30 MINUTES

- 2 tablespoons extra-virgin olive or canola oil
- 1/2 cup chopped onion
- 1 red bell pepper, seeded and diced
- 1 tablespoon minced garlic

In 12-inch nonstick pan, heat the oil over moderate heat. Add onions and sauté for 2 minutes, stirring occasionally. Add garlic, then pepper, and sauté 3 minutes longer.

- 2 teaspoons ground cumin
- 1 teaspoon crushed dried oregano

Add cumin and oregano and cook briefly, stirring.

- 1 15 to 16 ounce can black beans, rinsed and drained
- 1 tablespoon lemon juice
- 1 cup chopped fresh or canned tomatoes, drained, reserve juice
  Salt and pepper to taste

Stir these ingredients into the sautéed mixture and simmer, covered, for 5 minutes, adding water or tomato juice if needed to thin to desired consistency.

- 2 tablespoons dark rum
- 2 cups cooked white rice

Mix 1 cup of the bean mixture with rum and mash to a paste with the back of a fork or in a food processor. Add the purée to the pot set over low heat, cover, and simmer about 20 minutes. Serve over hot, cooked rice.

Serving suggestion: For more pungency, stir some chopped scallions, chopped hot chilies, and a little lemon juice into the rice. Sliced bananas on the side will help put out the fire.

BLACK BEANS AND TORTILLAS

This is one of our standby quick and easy recipes. It can be varied by whatever kinds of peppers, cheese, and surprises are available at the time.

PREPARATION TIME 20 MINUTES   **SERVES 4**

  1   cup long-grain white or basmati rice (see page 206)

Cook rice according to directions on package. As it cooks, proceed with rest of recipe.

  2   15 to 16 ounce cans black beans

Rinse the beans in a strainer and set aside.

  1   tablespoon peanut or extra-virgin olive oil
  1   medium onion, chopped
  1   large clove garlic, minced

In a wok or large nonstick pan, sauté onion for 1 minute, add garlic, and continue sautéing another 1 or 2 minutes.

  1   green, red, or yellow bell pepper, chopped
  1   teaspoon ground cumin
  1   jalapeño pepper, chopped—not too fine
  1   small tomato, chopped

Add bell pepper to pan and sauté 2 minutes more. Add jalapeño pepper and beans, then chopped tomato. Keep mixture warm.

  1   package store-bought 8-inch flour tortillas

Heat tortillas in microwave or oven, according to directions on package. Put between two cloth napkins on a plate to keep warm.

        Grated Cheddar or Jack cheese
        Chopped avocado
        Light sour cream
        Cilantro
        Hot sauce (optional)
        Nacho rings (optional)

We assemble the tortillas at the table: Spoon bean mixture and small amount of rice onto center of tortilla, top with grated cheese, avocado, sour cream, and sprigs of cilantro. If it isn't hot enough, add hot sauce and/or nacho rings.

BROCCOLI AND SPICY TOFU

You can make this dish mild or hot, depending on how much chile paste with garlic you put in. It's a dish that's great right off the stove and equally great two or three days after, so you can make it ahead.

PREPARATION TIME 20 MINUTES   **SERVES 4**

- 1   cup vegetable broth
- 1 to 2 teaspoons chile paste with garlic (available at Oriental food shops and some supermarkets)
- 1   tablespoon cornstarch
- 3   tablespoons tamari sauce
- 1   tablespoon Oriental sesame oil
- 1   teaspoon honey

Mix these ingredients in a food processor or blender and set aside.

- 1   pound broccoli

Peel stems and cut into ¼-inch slices. Separate head into small florets. Steam 4 minutes, or until barely tender. Set aside.

- 2   tablespoons peanut or canola oil
- 1   tablespoon minced fresh ginger
- ½   cup chopped scallions
- 1   pound regular or firm tofu, cut into ½-inch cubes

In a large, heavy frying pan, heat oil and stir-fry ginger and scallions for about 2 minutes. Add tofu and sauté, stirring gently, for 2 minutes. Add broccoli. Stir prepared sauce well and pour over the tofu and broccoli mixture. Reduce heat and cook, stirring gently until sauce thickens slightly. Serve over hot, cooked rice with crisp chow mein noodles on the side. Sliced orange or diced pineapple makes a pleasing accompaniment.

BROCCOLI WITH WATER CHESTNUTS

Frozen broccoli can be used in this recipe and requires no precooking. If you use fresh broccoli, steam it, covered, for 5 minutes, or until barely fork tender. Allow it to cool a little before chopping and adding.

PREPARATION TIME 10 MINUTES   **SERVES 6**
BAKING TIME 30 MINUTES
Preheat oven to 350°.

2	large eggs or egg substitute
1	cup low-fat cottage cheese
1	cup shredded low-fat Jahrlsberg cheese
3	tablespoons unbleached, all-purpose flour
1	teaspoon salt
1/4	teaspoon dried minced onion
2	tablespoons yogurt
2	10-ounce packages frozen, chopped broccoli, thawed
1	small can water chestnuts, rinsed, drained and sliced

Beat eggs slightly in a mixing bowl and stir in remaining ingredients. Pour in lightly oil-sprayed 9-inch baking dish.

Paprika

Sprinkle with paprika and bake for 30 minutes, or until firm. Cut into slices to serve.

BROCCOLI FRITTATA

Take your pick. You can make this recipe with eggs or egg substitute; the latter has the merit of being cholesterol free and 99% fat free. Read the label, and then decide.

PREPARATION TIME 15 MINUTES   **SERVES 4**
COOKING TIME 20 MINUTES

1	9- or 10-ounce package frozen chopped broccoli

Cook according to package directions. The microwave is the fastest way.

2	tablespoons unsalted butter
4	ounces fresh mushrooms, sliced
1	medium onion, chopped (quickest in a food processor)

In a 10-inch cast-iron skillet, sauté mushrooms and onions for 5 minutes, until tender but not brown.

>   2   large eggs and 4 egg whites, or 1¹/₂ cups egg substitute
>   ¹/₄   teaspoon salt
>   Freshly ground pepper to taste

Beat eggs or egg substitute and stir in cooked broccoli. Pour this mixture over mushrooms and onions; add seasonings. Cover pan and cook over low heat until the eggs set and are firm on top, about 12 to 15 minutes.

>   ¹/₃   cup freshly grated Parmesan cheese

Sprinkle the eggs and broccoli with the cheese. Put skillet under broiler about 6 inches from heat and broil for 2 or 3 minutes, until nicely browned. Cut in wedges and serve. Wedges come out of skillet easier if frittata is allowed to set a few minutes. Serve with your favorite tomato sauce or mild salsa.

BROCCOLI, NOODLES, AND RED BEANS

This versatile dish can be served hot or at room temperature. With the latter, it's good with cottage cheese. It's economical, too.

PREPARATION TIME 15 MINUTES   SERVES 4

>   1   tablespoon canola oil
>   1   onion (2 inches in diameter)
>   ¹/₄   teaspoon red pepper flakes (or to taste)
>   2   cups broccoli florets and stems

Sauté onion and pepper flakes on medium heat for 2 minutes, add broccoli (stems peeled and cut into thin slices), cover, and cook on low heat for 8 minutes.

>   1   cup medium-width noodles

Cook for 6 minutes in boiling, salted (1 teaspoon) water.

>   1   16-ounce can dark red kidney beans
>   Salt and pepper to taste

While noodles are cooking, rinse and drain beans. Add cooked noodles, beans, and salt and pepper to broccoli. Heat for 2 more minutes, or until all ingredients are warmed through and blended.

BUTTERNUT SQUASH AND PECANS

It's no problem to peel butternut squash. Cut it into quarters, remove the seeds and stringy pulp, cut each quarter into several pieces, and steam them, peel and all, over a small amount of boiling water for 15 minutes, or until fork tender. The skin will peel off easily then.

PREPARATION TIME 20 MINUTES   **SERVES 8 TO 10**

Preheat oven to 400°.

> **4** pounds butternut squash (about 4 cups cooked)

Place pieces of peeled squash in a large mixing bowl and mash, but don't try to make the texture supersmooth.

> $1/4$ cup unsalted butter
> 2 tablespoons finely chopped green onion
> 1 teaspoon dried rosemary
> $1/2$ teaspoon salt
> $1/4$ cup coarsely chopped pecans

In an electric mixer, beat the butter, onion, rosemary, and salt with the squash. Turn the mixture into an oiled $1^1/2$-quart casserole and sprinkle with the chopped pecans. Bake for 15 to 20 minutes.

Note: You can prepare this casserole, unbaked, ahead of time and refrigerate it, covered. When ready to use, bake.

BUTTERNUT SQUASH DELICIOUS

This is a wonderful addition to a holiday dinner, but you don't really need a special occasion to serve it. The succulent, golden, yet crispy-edged squash never fails to please.

PREPARATION TIME 10 MINUTES
ROASTING TIME 30 MINUTES
Preheat baking oven to 425°.

SERVES 6

    2   1¹/₂ to 2 pound butternut squash

To make the squash easier to peel and cut, cook them for 2 to 3 minutes in a microwave oven. Let them stand to cool off, then peel and cut them into 1-inch chunks.

    2   tablespoons extra-virgin olive oil
3 or 4 garlic cloves, cut into fairly thick slices
    2   tablespoons unbleached, all-purpose flour
  ¹/₄ teaspoon salt
       Generous grinding of pepper
  ¹/₃ cup grated low-fat Jahrlsberg or Parmesan cheese

Place squash and garlic in a bowl, toss with olive oil, then dust with combined flour, salt, pepper, and cheese until well coated. Place on a rimmed baking sheet (use two sheets if needed) and roast squash for 30 minutes, turning after 10. Transfer roasted squash to casserole, making sure to scrape up all the crusty bits clinging to the sheet. Keep warm until serving time. A sprinkling of chopped parsley or thyme is attractive.

CABBAGE AND MUSHROOMS

The rich, woodsy flavor of dried mushrooms, stir-fried with succulent cabbage and water chestnuts, then mixed with noodles, is an East-West combo that works.

PREPARATION TIME 15 MINUTES   **SERVES 4**

> 1   ounce imported dried mushrooms, any kind

Rinse mushrooms and cover with hot water. Allow to soak 15 minutes or until soft; drain, squeezing out liquid; and reserve soaking water. Discard stems. Slice mushrooms.

> 2   cups medium-width noodles

While mushrooms are soaking, cook noodles according to package directions, drain, and keep warm.

> 2   tablespoons unsalted butter
> 4   cups shredded cabbage
> 1   4-ounce can water chestnuts, drained and sliced
>   Salt and pepper to taste

In a large saucepan or wok, melt butter over moderately high heat. Add mushrooms and stir-fry for 2 minutes. Stir in cabbage, water chestnuts, and salt and pepper. Add 1/4 cup of the mushroom-soaking liquid (more if needed). Cover and cook, stirring occasionally, for 3 or 4 minutes. Add noodles, toss it all together, and serve.

CAULIFLOWER, LEEKS, AND NOODLES

Leeks are often expensive, but one or two large ones can go a long way, as they do here, to add incomparable flavor.

PREPARATION TIME 10 MINUTES   SERVES 4
COOKING TIME 20 MINUTES

    1   small head cauliflower
    1 or 2 leeks

Wash and trim cauliflower and break into florets. Cut off tops of leeks just above white part and trim off roots. Slash vertically, fan out leaves and wash under cold running water to clean out all grit and sand. Place cauliflower and leeks in a steamer basket over 1/2 cup of boiling water, cover, and steam 6 or 7 minutes, or until fork tender.

    2   cups broad noodles
    1   tablespoon unsalted butter or canola oil

While vegetables are steaming, cook noodles according to package directions. Drain, toss with butter, and set aside.

    2   tablespoons canola oil
    2   tablespoons unbleached, all-purpose flour
  1 1/2 cups skim milk
   1/3 cup cream or evaporated skim milk
   1/3 cup freshly grated Parmesan cheese
       Salt and pepper to taste
   1/2 teaspoon dried thyme

Melt the butter in the bottom of a heatproof serving dish until it is foamy. Stir in the flour and cook, stirring with a wire whisk for a minute or two. Slowly whisk in the milk, then add the cream and cheese. Cook, stirring for 1 minute. Season this sauce with salt, pepper, and thyme. Separate the leeks into individual leaves and add them with the cauliflorets and sauce to an oven-proof serving dish. Toss to coat with the sauce. Stir in the drained noodles and heat in 325° oven for 5 minutes, or until piping hot. Sprinkle with parsley and serve.

CAULIFLOWER, NOODLES, AND GREEN PEAS

This recipe works equally well with chickpeas (canned) instead of green peas. It's our favorite cauliflower dish.

PREPARATION TIME 20 MINUTES   SERVES 3 TO 4

    4   cups cauliflower (a small head)

Peel cauliflower stalk and cut into ¼-inch slices. Separate head into small florets. Steam for 6 minutes.

    2   cups wide noodles
    1   tablespoon canola oil
    1   cup chopped scallions (include all green)
    1   teaspoon vegetarian Worcestershire sauce
    1½ cups fresh or frozen green peas

Boil noodles in salted water until barely tender (usually 8 minutes). While noodles are boiling, sauté scallions in oil for 2 minutes, add peas, and cook until tender. Stir in the Worcestershire sauce; then add drained noodles and cauliflower.

    4 to 5 tablespoons pesto (buy, or see recipe on page 26)
    Salt and pepper to taste

Mix pesto with seasonings. Add to the cauliflower, noodle, and pea mixture and stir gently until well blended. At the table, offer freshly grated Parmesan cheese and a chunky salsa for topping. For bread, choose something dark and substantial.

CAULIFLOWER, RED BEANS, AND GREEN NOODLES

This dish can also be made with pea beans, lima beans, or chickpeas. But then it should include sautéed red pepper for color.

PREPARATION TIME 20 MINUTES   SERVES 4 TO 6

- 1 tablespoon canola oil
- 1 teaspoon peeled and chopped fresh ginger
- 1 teaspoon chopped garlic
- 1 cup water

In a large, nonstick pan, sauté the ginger and garlic in oil on medium heat for 1 minute. Add the water.

- 1 small head cauliflower, thinly sliced, broken apart

Add cauliflower to the ginger and garlic mix. Cover, reduce heat, and cook until tender, about 7 minutes. Remove 1 cup of cooked cauliflower for next step.

- 1 cup cooked cauliflower
- 2 tablespoons low-fat milk
- 1 teaspoon Oriental sesame oil

Blend cooked cauliflower with milk and oil in food processor until smooth. Return to mixture.

- 1 16-ounce can dark red kidney beans, rinsed and drained
- 1 tablespoon chopped fresh basil or 1 teaspoon dried basil
    Salt and pepper to taste

Add beans and seasonings to cauliflower, mix, and cook 1 or 2 minutes, stirring. Serve with a mild chile salsa over green noodles, prepared according to instructions on box. Corn is a good side dish.

CHILI CORN PIE

This mildly spicy pie is a welcome and warming meal on a cold evening. There is a definite flavor of Mexico in the crunchy crust and heartily satisfying filling. Combined with a crisp salad and a glass of red wine, this has become one of our favorite suppers.

PREPARATION TIME 12 MINUTES
BAKING TIME 25 MINUTES
Preheat oven to 350°.

SERVES 6

- 1³/₄ cups yellow cornmeal
- 3 tablespoons peanut oil
- ³/₄ cup hot vegetable broth
- ¹/₂ teaspoon salt

Mix cornmeal, oil, broth, and salt together with a fork until they form a doughy paste. Press into an oil-sprayed 8- or 9-inch pan to form a crust. Set aside.

- 1 cup chopped onion
- ¹/₂ cup chopped celery
- ¹/₂ cup chopped green bell pepper
- 1 tablespoon canola oil

Sauté onion, celery, and green pepper in oil for 2 or 3 minutes.

- ¹/₂ cup cooked corn, drained
- 2 cups cooked kidney beans, drained, liquid reserved
- ¹/₄ cup reserved bean liquid
- 1 6-ounce can tomato sauce
- ¹/₃ cup chopped peanuts
- ¹/₂ teaspoon oregano
- 2 teaspoons chili powder (or more to taste)
- ¹/₂ teaspoon ground cumin
- ¹/₄ cup sliced, pitted mammoth ripe olives
- ¹/₂ cup low-fat Jack or Cheddar cheese

Combine sautéed vegetables with remaining ingredients except olives and cheese. Spread ¹/₃ of the cheese on the surface of piecrust. Pour filling into crust and distribute evenly. Bake about 20 minutes. Remove from oven, spread sliced olives over the top, and cover with the remaining cheese. Return to oven for 5 minutes. Allow to cool slightly before cutting into wedges to serve.

COTTAGE CHEESE AND NOODLES—VERSION 1

There are dozens of cheese and noodle recipes around, but this one and the one following are our favorites. The first version has extra zip. The second version is superfast.

PREPARATION TIME 10 MINUTES
BAKING TIME 20 MINUTES
Preheat oven to 350°.

SERVES 4 TO 6

    3   **cups medium-width egg noodles**

Cook noodles according to package directions, usually for 8 minutes. Drain.

    1   **cup low-fat cottage cheese**
    1   **cup low-fat sour cream**
    2   **tablespoons minced onion**
    1   **clove garlic, minced**
    1   **teaspoon vegetarian Worcestershire sauce**
  1/4   **cup fine dry breadcrumbs**
        Dash of Tabasco sauce

Combine noodles with above ingredients.

  1/4   **cup freshly grated Parmesan or Cheddar cheese**

Place noodle mixture in 1¹/₂- or 2-quart casserole lightly sprayed with oil and sprinkle with cheese. Bake 20 minutes, or until heated through.

COTTAGE CHEESE AND NOODLES—VERSION 2
MICROWAVE

When you are in a *big* hurry, this is the recipe to use.

PREPARATION TIME 5 MINUTES
COOKING TIME 5 MINUTES

SERVES 4 TO 6

    3   **cups medium-width egg noodles**

Cook noodles according to package directions and drain.

    4 or 5 carrots
      Butter
      Salt and pepper to taste

While noodles are cooking, peel and slice carrots thinly. Put in a covered microwaveable bowl and cook on High for 5 minutes, or until tender. No water is needed. Add a dab of unsalted butter and salt and pepper if you like.

    1   pound low-fat cottage cheese

Serve cottage cheese with noodles and carrots at the side. That's it!

COUSCOUS AND CHICKPEAS

It would be difficult to find a delicious dish that is quicker and easier to prepare than this one. Its chopped apricots, crunchy nuts, and zesty jalapeños make it an incomparable treat you'll want to prepare time and time again.

PREPARATION TIME 10 MINUTES   **SERVES 4**
COOKING TIME 10 MINUTES

    2   tablespoons extra-virgin olive oil
    1   medium onion, chopped
    12 ounces mushrooms, sliced
    1   tablespoon reduced-sodium soy sauce

Sauté onions and mushrooms in oil over medium low heat in large nonstick pan until soft. Mix in soy sauce.

    2   cups vegetable broth
    1   cup quick-cooking whole wheat couscous
    1   teaspoon ground cumin
    1   teaspoon nutritional yeast (optional)
    1   teaspoon canned chopped red jalapeño peppers,
        or pinch of red pepper flakes
   ¹/₄ cup dried apricots, chopped
    1   16-ounce can chickpeas, drained and rinsed

Add broth to onions and mushrooms; then stir in couscous, cumin, yeast, jalapeños, apricots, and chickpeas. Bring mixture to a boil. Reduce heat, cover, and continue cooking until all liquid is absorbed, 3 to 5 minutes.

$^1/_4$ cup coarsely chopped pistachios or cashews

Sprinkle nuts atop each serving. A green vegetable or a salad with avocado makes a good accompaniment.

COUSCOUS CONFETTI

Couscous, a traditional grain-like pasta of North African countries, in this recipe combines beautifully with a legume; and the olives, pimento, and avocado colorfully underline its exotic origins.

PREPARATION TIME 12 MINUTES   SERVES 6
COOKING TIME 15 MINUTES

> 1   tablespoon extra-virgin olive oil
> 1/2 cup chopped onion

In a large, heavy-bottomed saucepan, sauté onion over moderately low heat for about 5 minutes, stirring occasionally.

> 1 1/2 cups vegetable broth
> 3   teaspoons chili powder
> 1/2   teaspoon ground cumin
> 1/4   teaspoon oregano
> 1   cup instant whole wheat couscous

Stir the broth and seasonings into the onion and simmer for 1 minute. Add couscous, stir, and simmer for 5 minutes.

> 1/2 cup sliced pitted mammoth ripe olives
> 1/2 green bell pepper, seeded and chopped
> 3   tablespoons chopped pimento or red bell pepper
> 1   16-ounce can red kidney beans, rinsed and drained

Stir above ingredients into onion-broth-couscous mixture, cover, and simmer until well heated through. Turn the mixture into a warmed casserole for serving.

> 1   ripe avocado, peeled, pitted, and sliced
>   Lemon juice
> 1/2 cup chopped cashews

Dribble lemon juice on avocado slices and arrange them decoratively on top of the casserole. Sprinkle with cashews. Serve at once or keep warm in a very low oven. Couscous Confetti is also good served at room temperature.

CURRIED CABBAGE AND TOFU

MICROWAVE

Chinese, Japanese, and East Indian influences are combined with modern microwave technology to produce a dish that is delicious in any culture.

PREPARATION TIME 5 MINUTES
COOKING TIME 10 MINUTES

SERVES 2 OR 3

1	pound regular tofu
1	tablespoon canola oil
1	tablespoon tamari sauce
1	teaspoon Oriental sesame oil

Cut tofu into $1/2$-inch cubes; stir-fry in oil for 5 minutes on medium-high heat. After 4 minutes, add tamari and sesame oil.

1	tablespoon canola oil
1	tablespoon unsalted butter
1	tablespoon curry powder
3	cups cabbage, thinly sliced
1	medium-size onion, thinly sliced

In a 2-quart glass casserole, heat oil and butter in microwave for 1 minute (High in 700-watt oven). Add curry powder to hot mixture and stir well. Add cabbage and onion and toss until coated. Cover and cook for 6 minutes. Add tofu around outer edge and cook another 2 minutes (3 minutes in lower-power oven).

Suggestion: Serve with potato, rice, or noodles and a salad.

EGGPLANT AND PEAS ITALIANO

Small Italian eggplants, olive oil, and Parmesan cheese give this pasta dish its special Mediterranean flavor. Peas provide color and fiber.

PREPARATION TIME 20 MINUTES   SERVES 4

Preheat oven to 425°.

    1   pound small eggplants
    1   tablespoon extra-virgin olive oil

Trim and wash eggplant. Cut lengthwise into 1/4-inch slices. Brush both sides of each slice with oil. Place in oven on lightly oiled baking sheet for 10 minutes, turn slices, and bake for another 5 minutes. Transfer to cutting board and cut slices into 1/2-inch pieces.

    1/2   pound frozen green peas

While eggplant is baking, place peas in microwave dish and cook, covered, for 3 minutes.

    1   cup elbow macaroni
    1/2   teaspoon salt
    2   tablespoons reduced-sodium soy sauce
    1   tablespoon mixed dry Italian herbs (oregano, basil, thyme)
    1/2   cup chopped onion or scallions
    1/4   cup freshly grated Parmesan cheese

Boil 1 cup macaroni in salted water until al dente, 8 to 10 minutes, and drain. Combine eggplant, peas, and macaroni. Add soy sauce and herbs to mix. Sprinkle each serving with onions and cheese.

Suggested accompaniments: Crusty bread, sliced tomato salad, red wine.

EGGPLANT PARMIGIANA EXPRESS

The usual procedure of sautéing eggplant in oil, after dipping it in egg and bread crumbs, is time-consuming and messy. Because each slice absorbs quite a lot of oil, it is also caloric. Here's another lighter, faster approach that yields delicious results.

PREPARATION TIME 10 MINUTES   SERVES 4 TO 6
BAKING TIME 30 MINUTES
Preheat oven to 425°.

> 1   medium-sized eggplant

Wash and trim eggplant. If skin is tender, there's no need to peel it. Cut into ¹/₂-inch slices.

> ¹/₄   cup low-fat mayonnaise (but not no-fat)
> 1   cup cracker or bread crumbs
> ¹/₃   cup freshly grated Parmesan or Cheddar cheese

Spread mayonnaise thinly on each side of eggplant slices and dredge in combined crumbs and cheese. Arrange slices on ungreased baking sheet and bake for about 15 minutes, or until browned and fork-tender. Reduce oven temperature to 375°.

> 1   thin slice mozzarella cheese for each eggplant slice
> 1   cup Quick Tomato Sauce (see below)
> ¹/₄   cup freshly grated Parmesan cheese

Layer the eggplant in a casserole lightly sprayed with oil, top each slice with mozzarella cheese, and sprinkle with half the Parmesan. Spread some of the tomato sauce on each slice and pour the remainder over all. Sprinkle with the remaining Parmesan. Bake (at 375°) for about 15 minutes.

QUICK TOMATO SAUCE

A quick tomato sauce can be made by diluting two 6-ounce cans of tomato paste with wine or water to make a thick sauce. Add ¹/₂ teaspoon basil, ¹/₂ teaspoon oregano, ¹/₈ teaspoon garlic powder, 2 teaspoons brown sugar, and salt and pepper to taste. If you have more than you need for this Eggplant Parmigiana Express, store remainder in refrigerator for later use.

FETTUCCINE WITH EGGPLANT SAUCE

All you need to complete this light repast is a salad, crusty bread, and perhaps a glass of Chianti.

PREPARATION TIME 20 MINUTES   **SERVES 3 TO 4**

    1   large eggplant (1^1/2 pounds)

Wash eggplant; then slash skin lengthwise and twice across. This will make it easy to remove flesh after broiling. Broil for 15 minutes.

    1   tablespoon extra-virgin olive oil
    ^{1}/2 cup chopped onion or scallions
    3   cloves garlic, minced

At medium heat, sauté the onions for 2 minutes; add the garlic and sauté for 1 minute. Scoop eggplant flesh from its skin and combine it with the onions and garlic.

    ^{1}/2 pound fettuccine

Boil fettuccine according to package directions.

    1   tablespoon extra-virgin olive oil
    2   tablespoons lemon juice
    ^{1}/2 teaspoon cumin
         Coarsely ground pepper to taste

With spoon, mix oil, lemon juice, and cumin with eggplant to make sauce. Add pepper.

    1   16-ounce can pea beans
    ^{1}/3 cup slivered almonds
    2   ounces feta cheese, crumbled

Drain and rinse beans, heat, and add to drained fettuccine. Add sauce and stir well. Serve with sprinkle of almonds and feta. For a final decorative touch, garnish with strips of red bell pepper.

FRIED RICE BALINESE

You can use almost any vegetables in making this dish. If you use leftover vegetables, they require less cooking. The result, in any case, is totally delicious.

PREPARATION TIME 20 MINUTES   **SERVES 4**

3	tablespoons peanut or canola oil
1/4	teaspoon red pepper flakes (or to taste)
1/2	teaspoon cumin
1/2	teaspoon turmeric

Heat oil in a wok or large, deep, nonstick frying pan. Add spices and stir-fry for 1 minute.

2	medium carrots, chopped or diced
1	red bell pepper, seeded and cut in 1-inch pieces
1	cup sliced mushrooms

Stir-fry vegetables over medium-high heat for 5 minutes.

4	cups cooked and cooled white or brown rice
1	tablespoon canola oil
2	tablespoons reduced-sodium soy sauce

Add rice, oil, and soy sauce to vegetables and cook, stirring constantly, for 3 minutes. Reduce heat.

1	tomato, cubed
5	scallions, sliced
2	Kirby cucumbers, sliced

Add above ingredients and cook for about 2 minutes, stirring gently. Push vegetable-rice mixture to the sides of the pan.

2	large eggs, lightly beaten, or egg substitute
1/2	cup chopped dry-roasted peanuts
	Lime slices, parsley, or coriander

Pour the eggs into the center of the pan and cook, stirring until they are just set. Stir eggs into rice mixture. Sprinkle peanuts on each serving and garnish with lime slices, parsley, or coriander.

FRIED RICE WITH TOFU AND ALMONDS

Cold rice is required for this dish, so prepare it ahead. It's a recipe that allows many variations; so if you want to experiment, feel free. But the following version is surefire.

PREPARATION TIME 20 MINUTES   **SERVES 3 TO 4**

- 1/2 cup chopped mushrooms
- 1/2 cup chopped scallions (include the green)
- 2   tablespoons peanut oil

Stir-fry the mushrooms and scallions for 3 minutes on medium-high heat.

- 2   cups cooked rice, cold
- 1   cup regular tofu, mashed

Add rice and tofu to mushrooms and scallions and mix well.

- 2   tablespoons reduced-sodium soy sauce (or tamari)
- 1/2 cup vegetable broth
- 1/2 teaspoon chile oil
- 1/2 teaspoon turmeric

Mix these ingredients together and blend with rice and tofu mixture, stirring until serving temperature is reached.

- 1/2 cup slivered almonds, chopped

Sprinkle 1/8 cup of the almonds atop each serving of fried rice. Serve with a mixed salad or green vegetable on the side.

GREEN BEANS AND CHICKPEAS

This is an old family favorite that we often serve with mashed potatoes. Rice, brown or white, is good, too.

PREPARATION TIME 10 MINUTES
COOKING TIME 25 MINUTES

SERVES 4 TO 6

    1   cup sliced onions
    1   tablespoon extra-virgin olive oil
    ½   teaspoon sugar

Sauté the onions over moderate heat until soft and golden, about 5 minutes. Sprinkle sugar over the onions while they're browning to caramelize them and give them a deeper color.

    1   16-ounce can crushed tomatoes
    1   tablespoon chopped fresh basil or 1 teaspoon dried basil
         Salt and pepper to taste

Stir these ingredients into the onions and cook for 1 or 2 minutes.

    1½   pounds fresh young green beans
    1   16-ounce can chickpeas, rinsed and drained

Trim green beans and cut in half. Add them and the chickpeas to the mix, cover, and simmer until are tender, about 20 minutes.

KASHA AND CHICKPEAS

If you are cooking for only one or two, make this complete recipe and you'll have enough for several meals. It keeps and reheats well.

PREPARATION TIME 20 MINUTES   SERVES 4 TO 6

- 1   cup whole kernel kasha (buckwheat)
- 1   egg white
- 2   cups vegetable broth

Beat egg white and mix with kasha. Stir the mix in a pan over medium heat until grains are separate and dry. Add broth. Cook, uncovered, for 10 minutes, or until all liquid is absorbed.

- 3   medium leeks, white part only
- 1   tablespoon extra-virgin olive oil
- 1   28-ounce can crushed tomatoes
- 1   16- to 20-ounce can chickpeas, drained and rinsed

While kasha is cooking, split leeks vertically and wash them carefully. Chop in food processor; then sauté in large, oiled skillet for 2 minutes. Add tomatoes, chickpeas, and cooked kasha.

- 1   tablespoon tamari sauce
- 1   teaspoon Oriental sesame oil
- 1   teaspoon vegetarian Worcestershire sauce
- 1   teaspoon dried thyme
      Sugar, salt, and pepper to taste

Add all seasonings to kasha-chickpea-leek mixture and continue cooking till tender. Serve with buttered noodles, green vegetable, and/or salad.

LASAGNE MIRACLE

This dish is a miracle because it's low in fat and high in protein and flavor and its noodles require no precooking. Several years ago, we gave up the messy, tedious job of precooking the noodles. The secret is to use extra sauce that has been thinned. The uncooked noodles simmer away in the sauce as the whole dish bakes, becoming tender and flavorful. This dish may be prepared for baking hours or even a day ahead. It can be baked and reheated; it can be frozen. It's a wonderful choice for a large group.

PREPARATION TIME 30 MINUTES   SERVES 8
BAKING TIME 1 HOUR
STANDING TIME 10 MINUTES
Preheat oven to 350°.

> 1   cup TVP© granules (we use "beef" flavored)
> 6 to 8 medium-sized dried Oriental mushrooms, broken into
>   small pieces, stems discarded
> 1   cup boiling water

Pour boiling water over granules and mushrooms. Allow mixture to stand while preparing sauce.

> 3   cups store-bought chunky-style tomato sauce
> 1   cup water
> 3   tablespoons tomato paste
> 3   cloves garlic, minced
>   A few drops Tabasco sauce (optional)
> 1   teaspoon dried oregano

Mix above ingredients. Add soaked TVP© granules and mushrooms and stir to blend. Set aside.

> 2   cups part-skim ricotta cheese
> 1/4 cup freshly grated Parmesan cheese
> 1   large egg and 1 egg white, lightly beaten

Stir well with a fork to make a smooth, spreadable mixture.

> 3   ounces part-skim mozzarella, grated or thinly sliced
> 9 to 11 lasagne noodles, or as many as needed to layer without
>   overlapping (You may need to break some.)
> 1/3 cup freshly grated Parmesan

In a 9-by-13-inch baking dish, spread a layer of sauce; add layer of uncooked noodles, then sauce, ricotta mixture, and mozzarella slices. Repeat noodle, sauce, and cheese sequence twice and end with sauce. Cover tightly with foil and bake about 1 hour. Check noodles for tenderness. When done, remove cover and sprinkle with Parmesan. Let stand for 10 to 15 minutes before serving.

LENTILS AND RICE

Remember the "mess of pottage" in the Book of Genesis that cost Esau his birthright? Well, here it is! We can't think why they ever gave such an unappetizing name to a dish that is so aromatic, savory, and delicious.

PREPARATION TIME 10 MINUTES   SERVES 6
COOKING TIME 45 MINUTES

- 1   tablespoon unsalted butter
- 2   tablespoons extra-virgin olive oil
- 2   cups sliced onions

In a 12-inch skillet, heat oil and butter until butter melts. Add onion slices and cook slowly, stirring occasionally. Increase heat to moderate toward end of cooking period to brown onion a little.

- 1   cup lentils, picked over and rinsed
- 5   cups water

While the onions are cooking, place lentils and water in a large saucepan. Bring to a boil, reduce heat, cover, and simmer for 20 minutes. Drain lentils and return them to saucepan.

- 3   cups vegetable broth
- 1/2   cup long-grain rice
- 3/4   teaspoon salt
- 1   teaspoon ground cumin
  A few grinds of black pepper

Add above ingredients to lentils. Reserve 1/3 cup of the onions and stir the rest into the lentil mixture. Bring to a boil, reduce heat, cover, and simmer for 25 minutes, or until rice is tender. Spread the reserved onions over the top and serve.

Menu suggestion: Baked potatoes and a simple tossed green salad complement this dish.

LENTIL-WALNUT PATTIES

Nearly everyone likes lentils. They can be used in many ways: in soup, as a hot vegetable, combined with other ingredients to make a main dish, or as a salad. These patties can be made with newly cooked lentils or with leftover ones.

PREPARATION TIME 20 MINUTES　　　　　　　　　　　　　　**SERVES 6**
COOKING TIME 10 MINUTES
Preheat oven to 400°.

　　2¹/₂ cups cooked lentils, drained

Purée the lentils in a food processor or blender, or mash them well with a potato masher.

　　2　cups walnuts
　　2　cups fresh bread crumbs

Spread the walnuts and bread crumbs on separate shallow pans and toast lightly in oven, about 10 minutes.

　　1　large egg, plus 2 egg whites, lightly beaten
　　¹/₂　cup finely chopped onion
　　2　tablespoons ketchup
　　¹/₄　teaspoon ground cloves
　　　　Salt and pepper to taste
　　　　Low-fat sour cream (if needed)

Chop the walnuts fairly fine in a food processor, blender, or coffee grinder. Blend walnuts and bread crumbs with above ingredients, adding a small amount of sour cream if mixture seems too dry. Shape into patties.

　　3　tablespoons canola oil

Sauté patties in oil over moderately low heat until nicely browned, about 5 minutes per side.

Menu suggestion: Good accompaniments for Lentil-Walnut Patties would be Lemon Parsnips (see page 203), spinach and raw mushroom salad, crusty rolls, and Fruit Mélange with Curaçao (see page 220).

MACARONI MIREPOIX

Mirepoix is a combination of finely diced carrots, onions, and celery sautéed in butter. Add it to a simple cheese sauce, fling in a bit of oregano, and *voilà*—you have an elegant macaroni and cheese. It's all done on top of the stove, which makes it great for campers, too.

PREPARATION TIME 10 MINUTES   SERVES 6
COOKING TIME 15 MINUTES

1   7- or 8-ounce package elbow macaroni

Cook macaroni according to package directions. Drain.

$^1/_4$ cup unsalted butter or margarine
$^1/_4$ cup shredded carrots
$^1/_4$ cup chopped celery
$^1/_4$ cup chopped green onions
$^1/_4$ cup unbleached, all-purpose flour
$^1/_2$ teaspoon salt
1   teaspoon oregano
2   teaspoons prepared Dijon mustard

While the macaroni is cooking, melt butter in a 3-quart saucepan. Drop in vegetables and cook, stirring, over moderate heat for 2 or 3 minutes. Add flour, salt, oregano, and mustard and stir well to blend. Cook over low heat for 2 minutes, stirring constantly. Remove pan from burner.

2   cups skim or low-fat milk

Stir in milk gradually, return pan to burner, and heat to boiling, stirring constantly. Boil and stir for 1 minute. Remove from heat.

$1^1/_2$ cups shredded low-fat Cheddar cheese

Add cheese to pan and stir until melted, returning pan to low heat if necessary to melt the cheese. Do not allow mixture to boil. Stir in the macaroni and heat to serving temperature.

Attractive garnishes: tomato slices and chopped parsley.

MEXICAN DOUBLE-DECKER   MICROWAVE

You can bake this Mexican-style tortilla treat in just 1 minute in a microwave oven. Though this recipe uses chopped onion, green pepper, and sliced black olives, you can also make it with almost any leftover vegetable, such as asparagus, or broccoli.

PREPARATION TIME 5 MINUTES   **SERVES 2**

6	8-inch flour tortillas
$^1/_2$	cup ready-made tomato or enchilada sauce
1	16-ounce can vegetarian refried beans with green chile

Place two tortillas on microwave dishes; spread with half the sauce and then with the entire can of beans. Cover each with a second tortilla and spread remaining sauce on them.

$^1/_2$	cup chopped onion
$^1/_2$	cup chopped green bell pepper
$^1/_4$	cup sliced pitted large black olives
$^1/_2$	cup shredded Monterey Jack cheese

Sprinkle the onion, pepper, olives, and cheese on the second tortillas and top with the remaining tortillas. Zap each double-decker for 1 minute. Cut each stack into quarters. Eat like a sandwich.

NEW ENGLAND PRESSURE-COOKED DINNER

How can we explain the fact that this simple dish is such an ongoing favorite in our family? Well, the flavors of the four vegetables do blend in an appealing way. And as wine experts might say of a wine, the vegetable combination is straightforward and unpretentious.

PREPARATION TIME 10 MINUTES   SERVES 4
COOKING TIME 5 MINUTES

4 medium potatoes, peeled and cut in 1/2-inch slices
4 medium onions, quartered
4 medium carrots, peeled and split lengthwise
1 1/2 pounds cabbage, cored and cut in chunks
1 teaspoon caraway seeds

Put ingredients in pressure cooker and cook for 5 minutes, until vegetables are tender. (Follow your pressure cooker instruction book for amount of water and how much food can be cooked at one time.)

Cottage cheese
Butter
Salt and pepper to taste

Add butter, cheese, and seasonings as desired to individual servings.

Note: Although cottage cheese is a favorite accompaniment, you may wish to try grated or shredded Cheddar, Swiss, Muenster, et cetera.

NUTTY NOODLE CASSEROLE

This casserole comes under the heading "Easy to Make, but Takes Time to Bake." It's worth the wait.

PREPARATION TIME 15 MINUTES
BAKING TIME 1 HOUR
Preheat oven to 350°.

SERVES 4

- 1 cup chopped cashew nuts
- 1 cup chopped onions
- 1 cup chopped fresh mushrooms
- 1 cup chopped celery
- 1 cup uncooked fine egg noodles
- 1 cup crisp Chinese noodles
- 1 cup vegetable broth
- 2 tablespoons canola oil
- 1/2 teaspoon salt

Mix all ingredients together, place in an 8- or 9-inch square baking dish that has been lightly sprayed with oil and bake for 1 hour. That's all there is to it!

ORIENTAL TOFU KABOBS

Tofu on skewers with an Oriental marinade is a weekend feast. The tofu and vegetables require time for marination, but you can go off to the tennis court or just sit in the shade with a good book while they do their thing, soaking up all the good flavors. The final result is lovely to look at and has a certain festive element in its presentation. It's a wonderful dish for guests, for it can all be prepared in advance, ready for the oven or grill. If you use bamboo skewers, soak them in water for 30 minutes before putting them on the heat.

PREPARATION TIME 15 MINUTES   SERVES 4 TO 6

STANDING AND MARINATING TIME 90 MINUTES

COOKING TIME 20 MINUTES

Near end of marinating time, preheat oven to 450°.

> 1¹/₂ to 2 pounds extra firm tofu

Drain tofu well. Wrap in a folded cotton towel and place on a rimmed baking sheet under a heavy skillet weighted down with something like a large can of tomatoes. Allow tofu to stand 30 minutes at room temperature (or longer in the refrigerator). Cut pressed tofu into 1-inch cubes.

> 3   tablespoons hoisin sauce
> 3   tablespoons Chinese rice wine or dry sherry
> 1   tablespoon tamari sauce
> 1   tablespoon minced fresh ginger
> 2   cloves garlic, minced
> 2   teaspoons sugar
> 1   teaspoon chile paste
> ¹/₂   teaspoon Oriental sesame oil

In a medium glass or ceramic bowl, whisk all ingredients together until well blended. Add tofu and stir gently to coat with the marinade. Cover the mixture and let it stand for 1 hour. Remove tofu from marinade and set aside. Reserve marinade.

> 2   red, green, or yellow bell peppers, or a combination, seeded and cut into 1¹/₂-inch squares
> 16 to 20 medium-sized fresh shiitake or other fresh mushrooms
> 1   large sweet onion, cut into wedges and separated into 2- or 3-layer pieces

Add vegetables to marinade and gently stir to coat them thoroughly. Place them in a bowl, reserving the marinade. Thread the tofu and vegetables on skewers, using as many skewers as necessary. Brush each skewer with marinade and lay them in a single layer on a large baking sheet that has been lightly sprayed with oil. Bake for 10 minutes. Turn skewers over and baste again. Bake 10 minutes longer, or until everything is tender and browned. Arrange decoratively on a large oval or round platter and serve.

Note: We often serve these kabobs with fried rice and a vinaigrette-dressed salad of sliced oranges, onions, and watercress or other greens.

MAKING PIZZA

Turning out a pizza need not take much longer than calling out for one, and you can make it exactly as you wish and know exactly what ingredients have gone into it. The most gifted pizza maker we know is a young man in Minnesota. We asked him how he does it, and here is his report, almost exactly as he wrote it, covering both the crust and three elegant vegetarian sauces.

THE PIZZA DOUGH

In a 1¹/₂-cup glass measure: 1¹/₃ cups warm water (quite warm, but not so hot that you kill the yeast), 2 teaspoons sugar, 1¹/₂ packets of quick-rise yeast. Let mixture sit until it's all puffed up, approximately 10 to 15 minutes.

Into the KitchenAid: 3 cups plus 3 tablespoons white flour, 1 tablespoon cornmeal. Use dough hook.

When yeast has risen, dump into KitchenAid and mix at 3 or 4 on speed control. When well combined, add 4 teaspoons extra-virgin olive oil and continue mixing. At this point, turn up mixer speed to 6. Whomp it good for about 4 minutes.

Remove dough hook and clean it off into bowl. Use rubber spatula and make dough into a ball. Add 2 tablespoons cornmeal and move dough ball around until completely covered and moving freely.

Place 1 square foot of wax paper over top of bowl and push it down till it covers the ball of dough loosely.

This has taken me about 20 minutes to this point.

Let the dough rise for 1 hour; then put it into the refridge until about 1 hour before you want to eat. I generally start making the dough at about 2:30 so that everything works out. Do you want to eat at around 5:45? Take the dough out of the fridge at 4:30 and prepare to roll it out.

First, I dump the wad of dough into my flour container to dust it. Sprinkle cornmeal on the *peel* (that wooden paddle for shoveling bread or pizza into the oven and taking it out). On the peel, roll the wad out with a rolling pin till it has a 15-inch diameter. Let it rise for 1 hour.

At this point, prepare a sauce, topping, and cheeses (specifics follow).

Preheat oven containing a large pizza stone to 475°. Prick dough all over with a fork, about 35 times. Bake it for 3 minutes. Remove from oven using paddle.

Spread sauce on with rubber spatula. Add toppings and cheeses. Put into oven and bake for 14 minutes, until cheese is bubbly and browned.

SAUCE 1

Cut a 1¹/₂-inch-thick ring of fresh pineapple and purée it in Cuisinart till smooth. Add 1 8-ounce can of Hunt's tomato sauce (no-salt-added variety), 2 tablespoons La Victoria taco sauce (mild green), 1 teaspoon ground cumin, 1 teaspoon basil, ¹/₂ teaspoon freshly ground black pepper, and 1 teaspoon low-sodium tamari sauce. This makes about double the sauce needed, so freeze half for next time.

The topping I chose for this sauce is red and green pepper, half of each. Cut into ³/₄-inch pieces, and with 1 teaspoon extra-virgin olive oil, sauté over medium-low heat, stirring occasionally, for 8 minutes.

SAUCE 2

Into the Cuisinart: 8-ounce can tomato sauce, 1 cup rinsed canned black beans, 1 tablespoon cumin, 1 teaspoon oregano, 1 or 2 cloves garlic crushed, 2 tablespoons mild green taco sauce (La Victoria).

The topping for this sauce: 1 medium onion and ¹/₂ red pepper, sautéed in 1 teaspoon olive oil on medium-high heat for 8¹/₂ minutes, stirring occasionally, until browned.

[Personally, we prefer this pizza with sautéed shrimp instead of the onion.]

Serve with plenty of coarsely ground black pepper; add red pepper flakes if you like the heat. Sprinkle a little chopped cilantro on top.

SAUCE 3

This is my regular sauce; I use it 99 percent of the time. In Cuisinart, combine 8-ounce can tomato sauce, 2 tablespoons La Victoria mild green taco sauce, 2 teaspoons cumin, 1 teaspoon dried basil, 1 teaspoon tamari sauce (low sodium, of course), ¹/₈ teaspoon sugar, 2 teaspoons salt-free Mrs. Dash.

Topping for this sauce: Peel a 1 pound eggplant and cut it into ³/₁₆-inch-thick circles. Place on a lightly oiled tray and bake at 425° until it's fairly dried out and a little browned. You'll need to flip slices once. Before using, cut into smaller pieces.

CHEESES

In a Cuisinart, use the metal blade to chop up the cheeses: 4 ounces mozzarella, 1 ounce medium (not sharp) Cheddar (If you don't have it, increase the mozzarella), 1 ounce Parmesan. Total cheese: about 1³/₄ cups.

I generally put some of the topping under the cheese, and some above—say, 50–50. It's pretty to have it on top, but if there's too much, the cheese is all covered and won't brown. Another tip: If you use pineapple as a topping, put it all on top. This will dry it out. Otherwise, it gets very wet under the cheese. Pineapple—we like this a lot. Don't even think about using canned!

Did I say how long to bake the pizza? At 475°, 14 minutes should just about do it. Remove from oven, cut pie up with wheel on the paddle, and then slide it back onto the stone, now placed on the table. Serve with crisp salad and beer.

Other toppings for Sauce 3: Mushrooms, but don't sauté. Put on top of the cheese (reduces their moisture). A large onion sautéed in 1 teaspoon oil 'til browned is good, too.

NUGGET, CORN, AND MUSHROOM STIR-FRY

The nuggets are ¹/₂-inch TVP© cubes, which are available in plain, beef, and chicken flavors, but which contain no animal products whatsoever. TVP© nuggets are available by mail order from Harvest Direct (1-800-8-FLAVOR) and Mail Order Catalog (1-800-695-2291). This is a hearty dish with a tangy flavor. Serve it over white rice, penne, or spaghetti.

PREPARATION TIME 20 MINUTES   **SERVES 4**

> 3   cups boiling water
> 1¹/₂ cups "beef" nuggets
> 2   tablespoons ketchup
> 2   tablespoons low-sodium soy sauce

Stir the nuggets, ketchup, and soy sauce into the boiling water. Reduce heat, cover, and simmer for 15 minutes. Set aside.

> 1   tablespoon canola oil
> 1   teaspoon Oriental sesame oil
> 1   cup sliced scallions
> 1   tablespoon minced fresh ginger
> 1   cup sliced mushrooms
> 1   cup whole-kernel corn
> 1   cup chopped celery
> 1   cup red bell pepper, cut in thin strips
> 2 to 3 cloves garlic, minced

In a wok or large frying pan, on medium high, heat canola and sesame oils, add scallions and ginger, and stir-fry for 2 to 3 minutes. Add mushrooms, celery, and corn, continuing to stir-fry about 4 minutes. Add peppers and garlic and cook for another 2 minutes. Drain nuggets and add to mixture.

> 1   tablespoon cold water
> 2   teaspoons cornstarch

Dissolve the cornstarch with water, add to wok mixture, and continue stir-frying for about 2 minutes, or until sauce thickens. Do not overcook.

PASTA PRONTO

Make this satisfying dish with your favorite pasta—spaghetti, fettuccine, rotelli, et cetera. Since it contains no tomatoes, you may wish to serve it with a lettuce and tomato salad.

PREPARATION TIME 5 MINUTES   SERVES 2

- **4** ounces pasta
- **1/2** teaspoon salt

Boil the pasta in salted water until al dente. If you use fresh pasta, you can have it ready in only 3 minutes. Williams-Sonoma has a dry egg linguini that cooks in 2 to 3 minutes; it has a shelf life of four to six months.

- **1/2** cup low-fat cottage cheese
- **6** pitted mammoth ripe olives, sliced
- **2** scallions, sliced (including green tops)

Place cooked pasta on a dish and put 1/4 cup cottage cheese atop each serving. Sprinkle olives and scallions atop cottage cheese. For crunch, add some chopped walnuts or slivered almonds.

PESTO, PASTA, AND POTATOES

Like many really good things, this recipe is simple. Easily made, and requiring only a few ingredients, it has a rich, spicy aroma that suggests the sunny coast of Italy. When baking potatoes, we always make a few extra to have on hand for recipes such as this. Pesto base takes only a few minutes to make in the food processor or blender and it can be frozen. Or look for it at your local supermarket.

PREPARATION TIME 20 MINUTES   **SERVES 4**

> 1   recipe pesto base (see page 26)
> 1/3 to 1/2 cup freshly grated Parmesan cheese
> 2 or 3 cloves garlic, minced

Stir cheese and garlic into pesto base. Set aside.

> 3   medium-sized baked potatoes
> 1   tablespoon extra-virgin olive oil
> 1   tablespoon fresh thyme leaves or 1 teaspoon dried thyme
>   Salt and pepper to taste

Cut unpeeled potatoes into 1/2- to 3/4-inch cubes and sauté in oil with thyme until nicely browned and crusty. Sprinkle lightly with salt and pepper and set aside. Keep mixture warm.

> 4   quarts boiling water, lightly salted
>   Handful of small, tender green beans, broken into pieces
> 1   pound fresh fettuccine

When ready to serve, bring water to a boil. Toss in the green beans and cook briefly until nearly tender. Add fettuccine and cook for 2 to 3 minutes more. Add 2 tablespoons of the pasta-cooking water to pesto and stir. Drain pasta and beans. Toss them with the pesto sauce and serve in individual warm bowls, topping each serving with the crusty, warm potatoes. Offer extra Parmesan cheese at the table.

POLENTA AND PEPPERED PEARS

Because Mother came from Romania, we grew up on *mamaliga*, the Eastern European name for polenta. In fact, we used to think that the "mama" in *mamaliga* referred to Mother. This was a hearty, staple food of the Slavic farmers, who ate what was plentiful and at hand—corn from the fields and cheese made from goat's milk. We've never outgrown our taste for *mamaliga*, but we have made a few changes in the traditional recipe.

PREPARATION TIME 5 MINUTES   SERVES 4
COOKING TIME 8 MINUTES

- 3   cups cold water
- 1   cup yellow cornmeal
- 1   scant teaspoon salt

In a 1-quart pan, heat 2 cups of the water with the salt. Mix the cornmeal with the remaining cup of cold water and add to the heating water when it boils. Turn heat down to low, stir cornmeal well, and cover. Stir once or twice as it cooks. It's done in 8 minutes and ready to eat, but we recommend you pour it into an oiled 8-by-12-inch pan, or equivalent, and allow it to cool. When cold, cut into 1-by-4-inch slices.

- 1   tablespoon canola or peanut oil
          Low-fat cottage cheese
          Fresh or canned pear slices, seasoned with freshly ground
          black pepper

Crisp the polenta slices in oil in a nonstick pan at medium-high heat. Serve with the cottage cheese and peppered pears. We like to decorate the plate with a daylily, nasturtium, or other edible flower when available.

POLENTA WITH MUSHROOM SAUCE

We usually make the polenta for this recipe a day or two ahead. It is much easier to cut when chilled and firm.

PREPARATION TIME 20 MINUTES   SERVES 4
BAKING TIME 20 MINUTES
Preheat oven to 350°.

 1   recipe cooked and cooled polenta (see page 171)
 1   teaspoon freshly ground pepper

Add pepper to the cornmeal mixture before pouring it into the pan. After cooling, cut firm polenta into ¹/₂-inch slices and then dice into ¹/₂-inch cubes.

 1¹/₂ cups tomato purée
 ¹/₂ cup light cream or half-and-half
 1   tablespoon tomato paste
 1   tablespoon chopped fresh basil or 1 teaspoon dried basil
 1   garlic clove, minced
     Tabasco to taste
     Salt if needed

Combine sauce ingredients in small pan and cook over low heat for 10 minutes.

 8 to 10 ounces fresh mushrooms (any kind), trimmed, cleaned
 1   tablespoon extra-virgin olive oil
 1   teaspoon vegetarian Worcestershire sauce
 2   tablespoons dry sherry

While sauce simmers, cut mushrooms into thick slices. Sauté them in oil over medium-high heat, stirring often, until they are tender and golden brown, about 7 minutes. Stir in Worcestershire sauce during last minute. Add sherry and cook until all liquid has evaporated. Add mushrooms to tomato sauce mixture. Spray an 8-by-10-inch baking dish with oil and arrange half of the polenta on the bottom. Spread half the sauce on the polenta. Repeat layers. Bake for 20 minutes, or until hot and bubbly. Provide grated cheese at the table for those who want it. Toasted pine nuts and chopped fresh basil leaves are an attractive garnish.

POTATO-ONION TORTILLA

We first ate this delicious Spanish tortilla in Jerez. In recent years, we've replaced its four eggs with one carton of packaged no-yolk, no-fat, no-cholesterol whole-egg substitute. The tortillas it makes are still a wonderfully quick lunch or dinner treat, and its calorie content is halved. It's good for breakfast, too. That's when we had it in Spain.

PREPARATION TIME 10 MINUTES SERVES 2
COOKING TIME 25 MINUTES

 2   tablespoons extra-virgin olive oil
 5   small unpeeled red potatoes, diced
 1   cup diced mild onion
 1/2 teaspoon dried oregano
 1/4 teaspoon dried thyme
 1/4 teaspoon cayenne pepper (optional)
     Salt and pepper to taste

In an 8- or 9-inch nonstick pan, sauté potatoes and onions until tender, stirring occasionally. Add seasonings.

 1   8-ounce carton defrosted egg substitute, well shaken

Spread potatoes and onions evenly in bottom of pan, and pour egg substitute over them. Cover pan, reduce heat to very low, and cook for about 15 minutes, or until tortilla is set. Loosen around edges, cover pan with lid, invert, turn tortilla out onto underside of lid, and slide it out onto serving board. This way, the browned bottom of the tortilla will be facing up.

Note: We like to serve the tortilla in wedges with a tomato salad that includes arugula, celery, dill, and other herbs and is topped by a sprinkle of feta cheese but no dressing. Also crusty bread. On occasion, we add some sliced mushrooms to the potatoes and onions as they near the end of their sautéing time.

QUINOA-CASHEW CASSEROLE   MICROWAVE

Quinoa (pronounced keen-wa) is a delicious, highly nutritious grain with an unusual flavor that has been described as "sweet" and "nutty." It has the highest quality of protein of any grain and has been a staple in Peru for centuries. You'll find it in natural food and gourmet shops.

PREPARATION TIME 15 MINUTES   SERVES 4
COOKING TIME 20 MINUTES

- 1   large garlic clove, minced
- 1   medium mild onion, chopped
- 2   tablespoons canola oil

Microwave above ingredients in an uncovered 2-quart container on High for 1 minute.

- 1   cup quinoa, washed in strainer under warm, running water for 1 minute
- 5   sun-dried tomatoes, chopped (not oil-packed variety)
- 2   cups hot vegetable broth
- 2   tablespoons tamari sauce
- 1   teaspoon cumin
- 1   teaspoon onion powder
- $1/4$ teaspoon cayenne pepper

Stir these ingredients into onion and garlic mixture, cover tightly, and microwave on High for about 4 minutes (or until mixture comes to a boil) and then on 50 percent until liquid is absorbed, about 8 to 10 minutes. Allow dish to stand, covered, for 5 minutes and then fluff mixture with a fork.

- $1/2$ teaspoon salt (optional)
- $1/2$ cup chopped cashews

Taste for seasoning and add salt if needed. Stir in cashews. Serve hot or at room temperature. This dish reheats well, so it can be made ahead.

Variation: Quinoa-Cashew Casserole makes a great stuffing for vegetables such as eggplant, zucchini, peppers, and acorn or butternut squash. We like to serve the casserole with corn on the cob or a baked potato and a zippy arugula or watercress salad with chopped Vidalia onions, chopped red bell pepper, and a few black beans tossed in. A simple oil and vinegar dressing does fine.

QUINOA, BLACK BEANS, AND CORN

This colorful, mildly spicy dish can be prepared completely ahead and reheated at serving time, so it's a great choice for a buffet.

PREPARATION TIME 20 MINUTES

COOKING TIME 20 MINUTES

SERVES 4

1 tablespoon extra-virgin olive oil
1 cup chopped scallions, including green part
2 cloves garlic, minced
1/2 teaspoon red pepper flakes
1/2 teaspoon cumin

In a heavy-bottomed 2-quart saucepan, heat oil and sauté onion, garlic, and pepper flakes, stirring occasionally, until onion is soft, 3 to 5 minutes. Stir in cumin.

1 cup quinoa, rinsed well, drained
2 cups canned diced tomatoes, drained, juice reserved
1 1/2 cups vegetable broth

Add quinoa, reserved tomato juice, and broth (there should be exactly 2 cups of liquid) to the sautéed onions and garlic. Bring to a boil, cover, and cook until the quinoa is tender and nearly all the liquid has been absorbed, about 10 minutes.

2 cups canned black beans, drained and rinsed
1 cup cooked corn (fresh, frozen, or canned)
1 tablespoon lime juice
2 tablespoons chopped cilantro

Add the diced tomatoes, black beans, corn, and lime juice. Stir together over medium-low heat until heated through. Transfer to an attractive casserole and sprinkle with coriander.

Suggestion: Serve with a basketful of soft, warm corn tortillas and a salad of avocado, romaine lettuce, and sliced oranges. Use a dressing of your choice.

RABE-TOFU-SOBA NOODLES   MICROWAVE

This dish has a tangy taste we find appealing. The rabe is loaded with minerals, vitamins, and fiber, and the tofu makes it a nutritionally complete and satisfying main course. You can use spaghetti, but we prefer soba noodles, which can be found in Oriental and natural food markets. Soba has a distinctive flavor and texture; and unlike spaghetti, it doesn't stick together after draining. Shiitake mushrooms are a zesty addition. This dish keeps well, so you can make it ahead.

PREPARATION TIME 20 MINUTES   **SERVES 4**
COOKING TIME 20 MINUTES

    1 to 1¼ pounds broccoli rabe

Rinse thoroughly and cut stems and leaves into ¼-inch slices. Set aside.

    1   pound regular or firm tofu
    2   tablespoons canola oil
    1 to 2 tablespoons reduced-sodium tamari or soy sauce
    ½   cup mushrooms, preferably shiitake, cut into ½-inch pieces

Rinse tofu and dry with paper towels. Cut into ¼-inch cubes. Oil a 12-inch nonstick pan and, on medium-high heat, stir-fry cubed tofu until most of moisture evaporates, perhaps 5 minutes. Sprinkle tamari over it, mix, and push tofu to edge of pan. Stir-fry mushrooms in center until tender, 3 to 4 minutes. Keep warm.

    ¼   cup extra-virgin olive oil
    ½   cup vegetable broth
    7 or 8 cloves of garlic, cut in half lengthwise
    ½   teaspoon red pepper flakes, chipotle puree or chile paste

Combine these ingredients in a 2-quart glass or china casserole and microwave uncovered on High for 3 minutes. Mix in rabe, cover, and microwave for another 8 minutes.

    4   ounces soba noodles
    1   teaspoon salt
    1   tablespoon freshly grated Parmesan cheese (optional)

While rabe is in microwave, boil soba in pot of salted water for 6 minutes; drain. Serve rabe mixture, reserved tofu, and mushrooms over the noodles. Sprinkle with a small amount of freshly grated Parmesan if desired. A sliced tomato adds color. Crusty French or Italian bread is a finishing touch.

Note: Chipotle peppers are smoked hot chile peppers usually packed in adobo sauce. They come in small cans and are available at Mexican and gourmet food shops. Purée contents of the can in food processor and then store in refrigerator in tightly-closed glass jar. It will keep almost indefinitely. It is very hot and has more character than plain red pepper flakes.

RICE PATTIES

These herb-flavored patties are crunchy and satisfying. They are a protein dish and go well with side dishes such as Zucchini and Cherry Tomatoes (see page 209) and Lemon Parsnips (see page 203).

PREPARATION TIME 10 MINUTES   SERVES 4
COOKING TIME 15 MINUTES

1   medium onion
1   16-ounce can red kidney beans, rinsed and drained
1   cup salted peanuts (add 1/2 teaspoon salt if unsalted)
1/3   cup sunflower seeds
1/2   teaspoon dried thyme
1/2   teaspoon dried sage

In a food processor, chop onions first; then add all other ingredients listed above and pulse until mixture is coarsely chopped and blended.

1   whole large egg
2   egg whites
1 1/2 cups cooked brown rice

Beat egg and egg whites lightly; add brown rice and all other ingredients. Mix well.

2   tablespoons canola oil

In a large, heavy-bottomed skillet, heat the oil over moderate heat. Make patties of the rice mixture by packing into a 1/3-cup measure, pressing it firmly into the measure with the back of a spoon. Drop the patties into the oil and flatten each one with a spatula into a round about 3 inches in diameter. Reduce heat to moderately low, and cook for 6 to 8 minutes on one side. Turn, cook 5 minutes on second side, or until golden brown, and serve. A dab of low-fat sour cream might be a welcome addition.

ROASTED VEGETABLES AND FETTUCCINE

Roasted vegetables have a rich, zesty, smoky flavor. You can use vegetables other than the ones we've named, but be sure they have equal roasting time. For example, potatoes, onions, carrots, and parsnips take longer. The vegetables themselves can be used as a side dish or combined with mozzarella in a sandwich.

PREPARATION TIME 20 MINUTES   SERVES 4
COOKING TIME 30 MINUTES
Preheat oven to 425°.

- 1   eggplant, about ³/₄ pounds
- 2   zucchini and 2 yellow squash, each 4 to 6 inches
- 1   large red bell pepper
- 1   large yellow bell pepper

Wash and dry vegetables. If eggplant skin is tender, do not peel. Cut eggplant, zucchini, and yellow squash into ¹/₂-by-2-inch strips. Remove seeds and membrane from peppers and cut into strips. Place everything in a large bowl.

- 2 to 3 tablespoons extra-virgin olive oil
- 2   tablespoons reduced-sodium tamari or soy sauce

Drizzle oil and tamari over vegetables and toss.

- 1   tablespoon minced dried onion
- 2   tablespoons vegetable broth powder
- 1   tablespoon onion powder
- 1   teaspoon dried thyme
- ¹/₄ teaspoon cayenne pepper (or to taste)

Combine above ingredients, sprinkle over vegetables, and toss to coat.

- 6 to 8 large cloves garlic, peeled
- Extra-virgin olive oil

Place garlic on a square of aluminum foil, drizzle with a few drops of oil, and twist edges of foil together to seal garlic inside. Lightly oil a large, shallow-rimmed pan (or two smaller ones) and arrange vegetables and garlic packet in it in a single layer. Roast for 20 to 30 minutes. Turn after 10.

- 4   ounces fresh shiitake or other mushrooms
- 2   teaspoons extra-virgin olive oil

While vegetables are roasting, stir-fry mushrooms in oil over medium-high heat until tender and nicely browned, 7 to 8 minutes. If mushrooms seem too dry after

5 minutes, reduce heat and add a little water or vegetable broth and cover pan. Transfer roasted vegetables to serving dish. Remove garlic pulp from foil; set aside. Add stir-fried mushrooms to roasted vegetables.

$1/4$ cup well-seasoned vegetable broth
1   pound fettuccine

Add roasted garlic pulp to vegetable broth and purée in food processor. Heat purée slowly while pasta cooks in boiling salted water. Place hot pasta in a large, warmed serving bowl. Pour on warm garlic purée and toss. Spoon warm, roasted vegetables over fettuccine and serve.

4   ounces crumbled feta cheese or freshly grated Parmesan cheese

Place cheese in a bowl and pass it at the table.

ROASTED VEGETABLE DINNER

This entrée is done entirely in the oven.

PREPARATION TIME 15 MINUTES   **SERVES 4**
ROASTING TIME 40 MINUTES
Preheat oven to 450°.

2   baking potatoes, cut as for French fries
     12-ounce eggplant, cut into $1/2$-by-$1/2$-by-4-inch strips
8   plum tomatoes, quartered
1   cup whole-kernel fresh corn or a 15- or 16-ounce can
1   cup cooked dark red kidney beans (or a 15-ounce can washed
     and drained)
2   tablespoons canola oil

Brush potatoes, eggplant, and tomatoes with oil. Arrange potatoes at end of a cookie sheet and bake in oven for 10 minutes. Arrange eggplant and tomatoes alongside potatoes and bake for 15 more minutes. Remove from oven and turn vegetables. Add corn and beans to sheet, brush all the vegetables with oil, and bake a final 15 minutes.

$1/2$ teaspoon onion powder
     Spicy ready-made tomato sauce
     Salt and pepper

Toss all ingredients together in serving bowl, adding onion powder, sauce, and salt and pepper to taste.

"SCRAMBLED EGGS" TOFU

Tofu scrambled-egg lookalikes can fill the same niche in your repertoire as the regular hen-laid variety—and without the cholesterol. How do you like your scrambled eggs: plain or with onion, cheese, sweet peppers, or mushrooms? Tofu is compatible with them all. Take your cue from this onion and mushroom version.

PREPARATION TIME 15 MINUTES   **SERVES 4**

- 1   tablespoon dehydrated minced onions
- 1   tablespoon water
- 1/2 teaspoon Italian seasoning
- 1/4 teaspoon turmeric
- 2   teaspoons vegetable broth powder
- 2   tablespoons tamari sauce
- 1/4 teaspoon Tabasco sauce

Mix these ingredients in a cup and reserve.

- 1   tablespoon canola oil
- 1/2 cup fresh shiitake or other mushroom, chopped
- 1   pound regular tofu
- 1   tablespoon finely chopped parsley
      Salt and pepper to taste

At moderately high, heat oil in 10-inch skillet. Stir-fry chopped mushrooms for 2 minutes. Reduce heat to medium and add tofu. Break it up with a fork. Add reserved liquid ingredients and blend thoroughly. Add parsley and salt and pepper if desired. Serve with potatoes and a garden salad or green vegetable.

Note: Italian seasoning is a blend of oregano, basil, rosemary, and various spices.

SPAGHETTI SIZZLERS

Next time you cook spaghetti, make extra. You can use the extra for these sizzlers. The recipe serves 1. Repeat the operation for each added serving.

PREPARATION TIME 5 MINUTES   SERVES 1

³/₄	cup cooked spaghetti
1	egg white (or entire egg if you prefer)
2	teaspoons reduced-sodium soy sauce
1	tablespoon freshly grated Parmesan cheese
¹/₂	teaspoon chile paste with garlic

Mix all ingredients thoroughly. Cook in medium-hot oiled pan, flattening mix to make a neat 6-inch cake about ³/₄-inch thick. In about 2 minutes, it will be ready to turn. Put a lid or plate over pan and turn pan upside down to remove cake. Return it to pan and do the second side. Mix and repeat for as many sizzlers as you want. They're especially good topped with a mild salsa.

SPICY ORANGE NUGGETS

This recipe uses "poultry" TVP© nuggets. If you can't get them at your local organic market, you can buy them by mail order by calling one of the toll-free numbers listed on page 29.

PREPARATION TIME 20 MINUTES   **SERVES 3**

1	cup "poultry" TVP© nuggets
2	cups vegetable broth
1	teaspoon rice vinegar or other mild vinegar
1/4	cup slivered organic orange peel

Boil the nuggets in the broth and vinegar for 5 minutes. Remove from heat. Add the orange peel, prepared by cutting peel crosswise into thin slivers 1-inch long. Soak 5 minutes.

2	tablespoons orange marmalade (Seville oranges)
2	cloves garlic, minced
1/2	teaspoon red pepper flakes
1/2	teaspoon ground ginger
1	teaspoon dried basil
1/2	teaspoon salt
1/2	cup orange juice

Add above ingredients to mix. Use additional orange juice if needed to facilitate blending.

2	tablespoons cornstarch
2	tablespoons water
1/4	cup dry sherry
1/2	cup cashew pieces

In a cup, mix cornstarch, water, and sherry; add this to nugget mixture. Bring to a boil, reduce heat, and stir until liquid thickens. Serve over white rice and sprinkle with cashews. For added decoration, use orange slices or mandarin orange sections. A green vegetable, perhaps broccoli, is a good complement.

SPINACH AND LOW-FAT SOUR CREAM

The little boy in the cartoon who said, "I say it's spinach and to hell with it," obviously must have had a traumatic spinach experience. Here is our blueprint for a spinach that may not be little-boy-proof but is delicious nonetheless.

PREPARATION TIME 5 MINUTES
COOKING TIME 8 MINUTES

SERVES 6

2   tablespoons unsalted butter
2   medium-sized onions, chopped
2   cloves garlic, minced

In a large skillet, sauté the onions and garlic for 4 minutes.

2   10-ounce packages fresh spinach

Wash and spin-dry spinach. Chop coarsely. Add to onions and garlic and sauté for 3 minutes. Remove from heat.

$^1/_3$ cup freshly grated Parmesan cheese
$^1/_3$ cup toasted wheat germ
$^1/_2$ cup low-fat sour cream

Blend these ingredients with the sautéed vegetables. Heat at low temperature until warmed through.

SPINACH LOAF

This is a traditional family favorite, and it is presented here virtually as it has been made down through the years. For extra time saving, use basmati rice, which cooks in only 12 minutes (see page 206); it also has superior flavor.

PREPARATION TIME 10 MINUTES   SERVES 4
BAKING TIME 20 MINUTES
Preheat oven to 325°.

2	packages frozen, chopped spinach, thawed and drained
1	cup cooked white rice
1	cup grated Cheddar cheese
1/2	teaspoon salt
1/8	teaspoon pepper
2	tablespoons ketchup
2	tablespoons prepared horseradish
1	tablespoon melted unsalted butter

Combine above ingredients and put in an 8-by-4-inch loaf pan sprayed with oil.

3	tablespoons bread crumbs
2	tablespoons minced parsley
1	teaspoon melted unsalted butter

Combine crumbs, parsley, and butter and sprinkle over the top of the loaf. Bake for 20 minutes.

2	hard-cooked eggs, sliced (optional)
	Tomato sauce, warmed (see page 151)

Serve garnished with egg slices (if you wish) and pass tomato sauce for topping.

SPANISH PILAF

A mélange of rice, vegetables, fruits, and nuts makes this pilaf a beautiful centerpiece for a summer buffet. The vibrant colors are straight from the Costa del Sol, and the fragrance is redolent of oranges and spices. Like all good buffet dishes, it can be made ahead and reheated.

PREPARATION TIME 15 MINUTES   SERVES 6
COOKING TIME 15 MINUTES

- 3 tablespoons unsalted butter
- 2 medium onions, sliced
- 2 cloves garlic, minced
- 1 red bell pepper, seeded and sliced
- 1 green bell pepper, seeded and sliced

In a large, heavy-bottomed saucepan, melt the butter over medium heat. Add onions, garlic, and peppers and cook, stirring, for 5 minutes, or until onions are tender.

- 2 large ripe tomatoes, chopped
- 1 seedless orange, peeled, sliced crosswise and diced
- 2 ripe bananas, peeled and sliced
- $1/3$ cup sliced or slivered almonds
- 2 tablespoons sunflower seeds
- $1/4$ cup raisins
- 2 teaspoons turmeric
- $1/2$ teaspoon salt

Add all ingredients to the pan and stir gently to combine. Cook, stirring occasionally, for 3 or 4 minutes longer.

- $4^1/2$ to 5 cups cooked basmati or other rice
- 1 mild sweet onion, thinly sliced and separated into rings
  Parsley or mint sprigs

Stir rice into the mixture and simmer, stirring occasionally, for 5 minutes, or until heated through. Pile the pilaf onto a warm, shallow serving platter and garnish with onion rings and herb sprigs.

Suggestion: Serve with rolls, a salad, and chilled white wine.

SUMMER SQUASH AND MUSHROOMS

When summer squash is plentiful, here is a good dish for a hot day. It works equally well with green or yellow squash.

PREPARATION TIME 20 MINUTES   SERVES 4
COOKING TIME 30 MINUTES

- 1   cup medium-width noodles
- 1/2 teaspoon salt
- 1   teaspoon extra-virgin olive oil or canola oil

Cook noodles for 8 minutes in boiling salted water; drain. Toss with oil; then set aside, covered, to keep warm.

- 1   tablespoon extra-virgin olive oil
- 2   cups squash, cut into bite-sized slices
- 1/2 teaspoon ground cumin

While noodles are cooking, heat oil in nonstick wok or 10- to 12-inch frying pan over medium heat; add squash, then cumin. Stir-fry for 4 to 5 minutes. Empty squash into a bowl and cover.

- 1   tablespoon extra-virgin olive oil
- 1/2 cup coarsely chopped scallions, green included
- 1   cup coarsely chopped mushrooms
- 1   tablespoon vegetarian Worcestershire sauce (or A-1 Sauce)
- 1   teaspoon nutritional yeast

In same wok or frying pan add oil, then scallions and mushrooms, and stir-fry till soft, 4 to 5 minutes. Add Worcestershire sauce and nutritional yeast, then cooked squash. Serve alongside a portion of noodles.

- 1   cup low-fat cottage cheese

Top each serving of noodles with 1/4 cup of cottage cheese. A sprig of parsley or dill on the cottage cheese is a pleasing final touch.

TOFU TEX-MEX

This is really a corn and beans recipe. The beans part comes from the tofu's soybean derivation. Serve over rice (basmati is nice) with corn chips on the side. *¡Olé!*

PREPARATION TIME 15 MINUTES   **SERVES 3 TO 4**

- 1   tablespoon canola oil
- 1   pound firm tofu, cut into ¹/₂-inch cubes
- 1   tablespoon reduced-sodium tamari or soy sauce

In a wok or 12-inch pan, stir-fry tofu in oil on medium heat until liquid evaporates and browning begins, about 5 minutes. After 4 minutes add the tamari. Set aside.

- 1   tablespoon canola oil
- ³/₄ cup chopped scallions, greens included
- 2 or 3 cloves garlic, minced
- ¹/₂ cup diced celery
- 1   cup whole-kernel corn
- 1   28-ounce can diced tomatoes, drained

Stir-fry scallions in oil on medium heat for 2 minutes; add garlic and stir-fry for 1 minute more. Add celery, corn, and tomatoes and blend well.

- 1   teaspoon oregano
- ¹/₂ teaspoon red pepper flakes
- ¹/₂ teaspoon ground cumin
-      Some coarsely ground black pepper

Sprinkle spices on tofu, add tofu to mixture and continue cooking for 2 or 3 minutes.

- ³/₄ cup Jack cheese, diced
- ¹/₄ cup chopped cilantro or parsley

Serve over rice. Sprinkle each serving with cheese and cilantro and place a handful of unsalted corn chips on the side.

TOFU, CORN, AND SAUTÉED POTATOES

Next time you bake potatoes, make two extra. They will be perfect, cut into quarters and sliced, for this recipe. Spinach Bombay (see page 207) is a fine complement to this dish.

PREPARATION TIME 20 MINUTES   **SERVES 3 TO 4**

Preheat oven to 350°.

1	pound firm tofu
1	tablespoon extra-virgin olive oil
2	tablespoons reduced-sodium soy sauce

Rinse, drain, and pat tofu dry. Cut into $1/2$-inch cubes and sauté in oil over medium heat for 5 minutes, turning occasionally, adding soy sauce after 4 minutes. Reserve.

1	tablespoon extra-virgin olive oil
2	baked potatoes, with skin, cut into $1/4$-inch slices, and quartered
2	cups fresh, frozen, or canned whole-kernel corn

In same pan in which tofu was sautéed, add oil and sauté the potatoes until lightly browned. Arrange in bottom of 8-by-8-inch baking dish lightly sprayed with oil. Spread corn on top of potatoes. Then add sautéed tofu.

1	pound can tomatoes, drained and diced
8	oil-cured olives, pits removed
1	tablespoon prepared horseradish
$1/4$	cup chopped parsley
1	teaspoon Italian herbs

Mix above ingredients and spread atop the tofu, working mixture down into corn and potato layers. Heat covered casserole in microwave for 2 minutes or in regular oven for 10 minutes.

Note: An easy way to loosen pits is to place olives in paper towel and pound with heavy pan or cutting board.

VEGETABLE, FRUIT, AND NUT CASSEROLE

To combine vegetables, fruits, and nuts is newsworthy, especially when the result is delicious. A colorful, nutritious, conversation-piece main course.

PREPARATION TIME 7 MINUTES   SERVES 4 TO 5
BAKING TIME 30 MINUTES
Preheat oven to 375°.

2	medium Golden Delicious apples, peeled, cored, cut into chunks
1	20-ounce bag of frozen mixed vegetables (any kind)
3	tablespoons toasted wheat germ
1/2	cup coarsely chopped walnuts
1/4	cup sunflower seeds
1/2	cup apple juice
1	tablespoon unsalted butter

Spray a 1½-quart casserole with oil. In it, combine apples, vegetables, and wheat germ. Sprinkle walnuts and sunflower seeds over mixture. Pour apple juice over all. Dot with butter and bake for 30 minutes.

VEGETABLE MEDLEY

This gathering of vegetables is rich in color, flavor, and texture. Though designed for easy top-of-range cooking, they end up in a casserole just for the sake of appearance.

PREPARATION TIME 10 MINUTES   **SERVES 4**
COOKING TIME 15 MINUTES

- 1   onion, chopped
- 1   green pepper, seeded and chopped
- 1   clove garlic, minced
- $1/2$ to 1 teaspoon dried oregano
- 2   tablespoons butter

Sauté the vegetables and oregano in butter for 5 minutes.

- 2   cups frozen mixed vegetables
- 4   cups thinly sliced zucchini

Add these to the sautéed vegetables, cover, and cook over medium heat for 10 minutes.

- 1   medium tomato, diced
- 1   cup grated Cheddar cheese
- $1/4$ cup toasted wheat germ
- $1/4$ cup chopped almonds
-      Mung bean sprouts

Stir in the diced tomato, half of the cheese, half of the wheat germ, and the almonds. Spoon into a casserole. Mix the remaining cheese and wheat germ together and sprinkle on top the casserole. Put under broiler for 1 or 2 minutes, browning lightly. Serve on a bed of mung bean sprouts.

ZESTY BEANS VERACRUZANA

You can use any kind of dried or canned beans. We like a mixture of several varieties.

PREPARATION TIME 25 MINUTES   **SERVES 6 TO 8**
Preheat oven to 325°.

- 1   **pound dried beans**
- 1   **teaspoon salt**

Wash beans thoroughly and soak overnight. Pour off water, add 1 quart of fresh water, the salt, and pressure-cook for 8 minutes. If you use canned beans, no preparation is necessary except rinsing and draining. Try one 16-ounce can of red and one of white.

- 2   **tablespoons extra-virgin olive oil**
- 1   **cup coarsely chopped green pepper**
- 1   **cup sliced onions**
- 4   **cloves garlic, peeled and sliced**

In a 12-inch pan, stir-fry the green pepper and onion in the oil for 3 minutes at medium-high heat. After 2 minutes, add the garlic.

- 2   **cups chopped fresh or canned plum tomatoes with liquid**
- $^1/_2$ **teaspoon ground coriander**
- $^1/_2$ **teaspoon dried basil**
- 1   **tablespoon chili powder**
- 1   **teaspoon sugar**
-     **Juice of 1 lemon or lime**

Mix seasonings and tomatoes with beans; cook for 6 to 8 minutes. Transfer to large baking dish and heat in oven for 15 minutes before serving. Decorate with sliced stuffed olives and cilantro leaves. Rice or tortillas are good on the side.

ZUCCHINI STUFFED WITH MUSHROOMS AND ALMONDS

We often choose this dish when we are invited to a potluck dinner party and asked to "bring something for the vegetarians." It's easy to do but apparently looks as if it required some effort. Everyone—vegetarians and non—seems to enjoy it, so we always make plenty. It's also a children's favorite; they call them "zucchini boats." One grandson, who is now thirteen, has ordered them for his birthday dinner for the last five or six years.

The zucchini can be prepared up to the point of final baking and refrigerated as much as a day ahead. Once they're baked, it's best not to reheat them because the zucchini shells may become soft and limp, making them difficult to serve. If you're taking them with you, try to arrange to bake them after your arrival.

PREPARATION TIME 25 MINUTES   SERVES 8
BAKING TIME 20 TO 25 MINUTES
Preheat oven to 400°.

  4   large zucchini, 7 to 8 inches long

Wash zucchini, trim off the ends, and cut in half lengthwise. Steam over 1 inch of boiling salted water for 4 minutes. Remove from steamer with tongs and plunge immediately into cold water. Drain, cut side down, on paper towels. With a grapefruit spoon or tablespoon, scoop out a trough in each squash half to hold the filling. Chop the scooped-out pulp, squeeze very dry between paper towels, and set aside.

  2   tablespoons unsalted butter
  2   scallions, minced, including green part
  1   cup finely chopped fresh mushrooms, squeezed dry between paper
       towels
  1   clove garlic, crushed
       Chopped zucchini pulp

Melt butter in a heavy skillet over low heat and sauté the onions, covered, for about 5 minutes. Uncover, raise heat to moderately high, and add the garlic, chopped zucchini, and mushrooms. Sauté for 2 or 3 minutes longer. Remove from heat.

  $^1/_3$ cup grated low-fat Swiss cheese
  $^1/_2$ cup almonds (ground in blender or food processor)
  $^1/_2$ cup dry bread crumbs (or more)
  $^1/_4$ teaspoon ground cloves
       Salt and pepper to taste

Stir all ingredients into filling mixture.

1   large egg or egg substitute
$^1/_2$ cup low-fat sour cream

Beat egg and sour cream together and blend into the filling mixture. Mixture should be thick enough to mound up when spooned into zucchini shells. If not, add more crumbs.

$^1/_4$ cup dry bread crumbs
     Melted unsalted butter

Arrange zucchini shells in oil-sprayed shallow baking dish large enough to hold them in one layer. Heap the stuffing into each half. Mix bread crumbs and butter and sprinkle over tops. Bake for 20 to 25 minutes.

ZUCCHINI PANCAKES

Zucchini is one of the ever-present vegetables. It's available all year in the markets, and during the summer months home gardeners sometimes find themselves knee-deep in a "zucchini problem." What to do with all that squash? Make zucchini pancakes.

PREPARATION TIME 15 MINUTES   SERVES 4
COOKING TIME 4 TO 7 MINUTES

> 2   medium-sized zucchini, grated
> 1/4 cup chopped onion
> 1/2 teaspoon salt

Toss zucchini and onion with salt and let stand 10 minutes.

> 2   large eggs, lightly beaten
> 1/2 teaspoon salt
> 1   tablespoon chopped fresh basil or 1 teaspoon dried basil
>   Freshly ground black pepper to taste

In a large bowl, combine above ingredients. With a potato ricer, press liquid from zucchini and onion; then stir them in with eggs.

> Fine bread or cracker crumbs (as needed)

Stir in crumbs until mixture holds together.

> 1   tablespoon unsalted butter
> 2   tablespoons canola oil

In a large, heavy skillet, heat butter and oil. When hot, drop in batter in large spoonfuls (an ice-cream scoop works beautifully) and flatten each cake slightly. Cook until crisp and brown on each side.

> Low-fat sour cream

Serve pancakes with sour cream. They are also excellent with Tomatoes With a Golden Topping (see page 208) and corn on or off the cob.

ZUCCHINI, TOMATOES, AND TOFU

This is a good dish to make during the summer, when zucchini and tomatoes are flooding the market. The spices add an unusual, pleasant zing.

PREPARATION TIME 15 MINUTES
BAKING TIME 20 MINUTES
Preheat oven to 350°.

SERVES 4

3	medium zucchini
2	tomatoes

Remove the stem and blossom ends and cut the zucchini into ¼-inch slices. Cut tomatoes into 1-inch chunks.

1	pound firm tofu

Rinse, drain, and dry tofu well. Slice into thin strips 1 inch wide. Place tofu slices on oiled-sprayed cookie sheet under broiler for 4 minutes, turning after 2 minutes.

½	cup low-fat mayonnaise
2	teaspoons vegetarian Worcestershire sauce
1	tablespoon Dijon mustard
1	teaspoon curry powder
1	teaspoon grated fresh gingerroot or ½ teaspoon ground ginger
½	cup toasted wheat germ
½	cup grated Jack cheese

Combine the mayonnaise, Worcestershire, mustard, and other spices. Spray an 8-by-10-inch baking dish with oil; layer half the zucchini, tomatoes, and tofu and spread with half the mayonnaise mixture and wheat germ. Repeat the layers, in the same order, with the second half of the ingredients, ending with the mayonnaise mixture and wheat germ. Sprinkle with the cheese. Bake for 20 minutes.

Vegetable Side Dishes

There are those who believe that vegetables require only butter, salt, and pepper and that this is the quickest and easiest way to prepare them. Playing devil's advocate, we'll answer that it would be even quicker and easier to eat them without this seasoning. However, if you are trying to enhance the vegetable's taste, why not anise on carrots, cumin on potatoes, dill on cauliflower?

The quickest and easiest way to prepare artichokes is in the microwave. Two large artichokes can be cooked in 10 minutes.

PREPARATION TIME 5 MINUTES

SERVES 2

COOKING TIME 10 MINUTES

2   artichokes

Wash artichokes, trim end of stems, and discard small, lower leaves (they're bitter). Cut each artichoke in half crosswise and discard top half. With a grapefruit knife, make a circular cut and remove dense interior leaves and fuzz. A grapefruit spoon is a good scraping tool, especially for the fuzz.

8   large garlic cloves (or more)

At least four large cloves are needed for each artichoke. Cut each clove into thin slices. Insert slices into spaces between leaves. The more garlic you can insert, the better. Put both garlic-stuffed artichokes into a 2-quart microwave casserole, add 2 tablespoons of water, cover, and cook on High until tender, usually about 10 minutes.

Artichokes are eaten by pulling off each leaf, inserting the thick end between teeth, and scraping off the soft meat. Many people prefer to dip the meat end in melted butter before eating, but it is certainly not essential. The garlic is especially delicious.

CARROTS WITH ANISEED

Anise is a sweet-smelling herb related to the carrot family. Maybe this kinship accounts for the fact that carrots and the seeds of the anise plant go together so beautifully.

PREPARATION TIME 4 TO 6 MINUTES   SERVES 4
COOKING TIME 12 TO 15 MINUTES

$1^1/_2$ pounds carrots

Peel carrots. If they are large, halve or quarter them to approximate the size of small carrots. Pressure-cook the carrots until tender, usually about 4 minutes. Drain and dry. To dry, put pot over hot burner and shake.

2   tablespoons unsalted butter
1   tablespoon brown sugar
$^1/_2$ teaspoon whole aniseed
$^1/_2$ teaspoon freshly ground black pepper

In a large, ovenproof nonstick skillet, melt the butter over moderate heat and stir in the sugar, aniseed, and pepper. Add the carrots and stir to coat well. Put carrots under broiler, turning occasionally, until they are glazed and have turned a deep, rich color.

CAULIFLOWER WITH SESAME SEEDS

In this recipe, toasted sesame seeds, green onion, and sweet pepper add piquancy to the cauliflower's flavor.

PREPARATION TIME 10 MINUTES   SERVES 6
COOKING TIME 12 MINUTES

1   head cauliflower
1   teaspoon lemon juice

Separate cauliflower into florets and steam over 1 inch of boiling water to which you have added the lemon juice. Cook until barely tender when pierced, about 10 minutes.

2   tablespoons canola oil
3   tablespoons chopped onion
2   tablespoons Dijon mustard

While cauliflower steams, heat the oil in a large, heavy frying pan and sauté the onion until soft. Add mustard and then the steamed cauliflower, stirring gently to combine.

4   tablespoons sesame seeds

Toast seeds in a dry skillet over very low heat for 1 or 2 minutes only, shaking the pan to toast the seeds evenly.

¹/₃ cup chopped green onions
¹/₃ cup chopped red and/or green bell pepper
     Salt and pepper to taste

Stir these ingredients into the cauliflower mix and cook for 1 minute, just long enough to heat through and blend flavors.

CORN IN 3 MINUTES   MICROWAVE

In most microwave ovens (700 watts or better), it takes just 3 minutes to cook one ear of corn, 5 minutes for two. If you have more ears than that, you may do just as well to boil or roast them.

PREPARATION TIME 1 MINUTE   SERVES 1

1   ear of corn

Trim off both ends of the ear. Peel away the 4 or 5 exterior husks but leave enough to cover the kernels. Microwave on High for 3 minutes. When corn has cooled enough to handle, remove remaining husks. Remove silk by rubbing with paper towel.

FRENCH FRIES WITHOUT FRYING

They're roasted, not fried. They're fat-free and totally delicious!

PREPARATION TIME 10 MINUTES   SERVES 4
BAKING TIME 30 MINUTES
Preheat oven to 425°.

- 4 medium baking potatoes, peeled
- 1 lightly beaten egg white
  Salt and pepper to taste

Cut each potato lengthwise into 8 pieces and brush the wedges with the egg white. Place the potatoes on an oil-sprayed baking sheet and sprinkle them lightly with salt and pepper. Bake for about 30 minutes, turning the slices several times during roasting period, until they are crusty and golden.

GREEN BEANS AMANDINE

This recipe produces a crisp, multiflavored green bean unlike the standard green bean side dish.

PREPARATION TIME 10 MINUTES   SERVES 4 TO 6
COOKING TIME 7 TO 10 MINUTES

- 1 pound green beans

Cut off ends of beans and wash. Snap beans in half. Steam beans until crisp tender, 2 to 6 minutes, depending on their size and maturity. Rinse with cold water to stop further cooking. Drain well.

- 2 tablespoons unsalted butter
- 1 clove garlic, minced
- 1 teaspoon each oregano and basil (1 tablespoon if you use minced fresh herbs)
- ½ cup sliced almonds
  Salt and pepper to taste

Melt butter in heavy nonstick skillet, add garlic and herbs, and stir 1 minute. Add almonds and cook for 1 minute. Add green beans and cook until heated through. Add salt and pepper as desired.

LEMON PARSNIPS

Parsnips have a rather sweet, yet slightly pungent taste that blends well with lemon. When they're steamed in butter until just tender, with crisp, brown edges here and there, and laced with lemon juice, they become a vegetable to cherish. See what you think.

PREPARATION TIME 5 MINUTES   SERVES 4
COOKING TIME 9 MINUTES

1	pound parsnips
3	tablespoons unsalted butter
6	tablespoons vegetable stock

Cut off ends of parsnips and peel with a swivel peeler. Cut into 1/4-inch crosswise slices. In a medium-sized skillet with a lid, melt butter over moderately high heat. Add parsnips and toss to coat with butter. Pour in stock. Cover, bring to a boil and steam about 7 minutes, stirring once or twice, or shaking pan to keep parsnips from sticking.

2	tablespoons lemon juice
	Salt and pepper

Just before serving, stir in lemon juice, season with salt and pepper and toss over high heat for a few minutes until piping hot.

OVERNIGHT SUCCESS PICKLES

These easy pickles require no cooking or processing and are kept in the refrigerator. Fresh-tasting, crisp, and sweetened with honey, they will keep for several weeks, but we doubt they will be around that long. Choose cucumbers that are firm, fresh, and long in proportion to their circumference; Kirbies are a good choice.

PREPARATION TIME 12 MINUTES   MAKES ABOUT 1 QUART
PLUS STANDING TIME

3   large cucumbers, about 1½ inches in diameter, or 7 or 8
    pickle-size Kirbies
1   medium onion, chopped
1   red or green bell pepper, stemmed, seeded, chopped
1   tablespoon kosher or other noniodized salt
2   teaspoons celery seed

If cucumbers have been waxed, peel them. Otherwise scrub them well and slice thinly. In a large bowl, stir together cucumbers, onion, pepper, salt, and celery seed until well combined. Let stand 1 hour.

½   cup honey
½   cup distilled white vinegar

Thoroughly mix honey and vinegar. Pour over pickles and stir to blend. Place in a covered glass container and refrigerate. Pickles are ready to eat in 24 hours.

PEAS AND KASHA

An unusual combination with a pleasing result.

PREPARATION TIME 5 MINUTES   SERVES 4 TO 6
COOKING TIME 5 MINUTES

3   cups water
½   teaspoon salt
1   medium onion, chopped
2   tablespoons butter

Put salted water on high heat. While waiting for water to boil, sauté the onion for 4 or 5 minutes.

1 cup medium kasha (roasted buckwheat kernels)
1 cup frozen peas
  Low-sodium soy sauce

Pour kasha into boiling water, lower heat, and cook, covered, for 5 minutes. A minute before kasha is done, stir in the frozen peas and sautéed onions. Add soy sauce to taste.

PERUVIAN LIMAS

Lima beans originated in South America and are named for the capital of Peru. We have no idea what herbs pre-Columbian cooks might have used to accentuate the rich, distinctive flavor of their beans, but here's a combination we like.

PREPARATION TIME 10 MINUTES   SERVES 4
COOKING TIME 15 MINUTES

2 10-ounce packages frozen lima beans

Cook beans according to package directions.

2 tablespoons unsalted butter
1 tablespoon chopped shallots, chives, or scallions (white and green parts)

In a large saucepan, melt butter and sauté shallots until soft.

1 teaspoon lemon juice
1 tablespoon chopped parsley
1 teaspoon dried tarragon or 1 tablespoon fresh tarragon

Add these ingredients to shallots and stir in beans.

¼ cup sautéed sliced mushrooms, or 1 tablespoon Duxelles (see page 25)

Add mushrooms or Duxelles to beans, cover, and simmer until heated through.

RICE AND PEAS CURRY

At your supermarket, you'll find instant brown rice. It cooks in just 10 minutes, which makes it perfect for this 10-minute recipe.

PREPARATION TIME 10 MINUTES   **SERVES 4**
COOKING TIME 10 MINUTES

1	medium onion, chopped
2	tablespoons extra-virgin olive oil
$1/2$	teaspoon curry powder (Madras preferred)

Sauté onion for 5 minutes, stirring to combine with curry powder. Almost simultaneously, you can start the second half of the recipe.

4	cups cooked brown rice
$1^1/2$	cups frozen green peas
	Salt and pepper to taste

Add these ingredients to the sautéed onion and heat through. The dish is ready to serve.

RICE—BROWN, WHITE, AND BASMATI

Brown rice is richer in nutrients. It has the drawback of cooking slowly, typically 45 minutes, but there are ways around this. Soak it for 5 hours or overnight, and it will cook in 20 minutes. Another good ploy is to cook it in a large quantity and refrigerate what you don't need immediately. It will keep about a week. You can also freeze what you don't need in cup-size containers. It will keep for several months. Defrost it in about 5 minutes in the oven or on the stove top or about 1 minute in the microwave. Add 2 tablespoons of water per cup of rice.

You can buy packaged "instant" brown rices that cook in 10 to 12 minutes. Typically, the outer husk has been removed and the rice has been steamed.

Basmati rice has the reputation of being the most delicate, aromatic, and delicious of all. It comes in both brown and white. It is faster cooking than other rice varieties.

White basmati can be cooked in as little as 10 minutes, compared with 20 minutes for regular white. The technique is to boil it in a large amount of water, which is then drained off. Here's how.

PREPARATION TIME 5 MINUTES   MAKES 3 CUPS
COOKING TIME 10 TO 12 MINUTES

- 1   cup white basmati rice
- 6   cups water
- ¹/₂ teaspoon salt

Wash rice in a tilted saucepan under running water until water is clear. Drain well. Bring water and salt to boiling point; add rice. Boil, uncovered, for 10 to 12 minutes, or until done; then drain. Simple, isn't it?

SPINACH BOMBAY

Here's a simple but sophisticated way to prepare spinach. The spices give it an East Indian nuance.

PREPARATION TIME 5 MINUTES   SERVES 2
COOKING TIME 5 MINUTES

- 1   pound fresh spinach

Wash, drain well, trim if required, and chop coarsely.

- 3   tablespoons canola oil
- ¹/₂ teaspoon ground cumin
- ¹/₄ teaspoon cayenne
       Pinch of salt

In a large pot warm oil over moderate heat; stir in cumin, cayenne, and salt. Add spinach to oil and seasonings and toss to coat leaves. Cover pot and cook over low heat for 3 minutes, or until spinach is completely wilted.

TOMATOES WITH A GOLDEN TOPPING

Ripe tomatoes can be delicious when simply sprinkled with some chopped herbs, salt, pepper, and a little oil and broiled for about 5 minutes. For a change, though, you might like to try them with this puffy golden topping.

PREPARATION TIME 5 MINUTES   **SERVES 6**
BROILING TIME 5 MINUTES

> 6   firm, ripe tomatoes
>   Salt and pepper

Core tomatoes and slice them in half horizontally. Oil-spray a shallow pan or dish large enough to hold the tomatoes in one layer. Arrange the slices cut side up. Sprinkle with salt and pepper.

> $^1/_2$ cup low-fat mayonnaise (not no-fat)
> $^1/_2$ cup freshly grated Parmesan cheese
> 4   scallions, green part only, finely chopped

Mix ingredients together with a fork. Spread a generous amount of mayonnaise mixture on each tomato half. Place under broiler and broil until puffed, bubbly, and golden. Serve immediately.

ZUCCHINI WITH CHERRY TOMATOES

This dish will be at its best if you can find small, young zucchini. For superior flavor and appearance, it should be made just before serving.

PREPARATION TIME 10 MINUTES   **SERVES 6 TO 8**
COOKING TIME 6 MINUTES

1¹/₂ **pounds zucchini**

Cut zucchini into ¹/₂-inch slices. Steam them over 1 inch of boiling water until barely tender, about 5 minutes. Drain well.

3   **tablespoons unsalted butter**
2   **cups cherry tomatoes, halved**
1   **teaspoon salt**
1   **teaspoon dried basil**
    Freshly ground pepper

Melt butter in a large, heavy skillet. Add zucchini and remaining ingredients, toss gently and taste for seasoning. Simmer about 1 minute, or until the tomatoes are heated.

1   **tablespoon toasted sesame seeds**
2   **tablespoons chopped parsley**

Add seeds and parsley, toss, and serve.

Desserts

Almost any dessert is a vegetarian dessert, so the field is wide open. Enjoy yourself! However, not all desserts suit the desires of those who sometimes wish to limit their intake of fat and calories. Most of the desserts in this section do fulfill those requirements. We hope you'll find them enjoyable as well.

Is someone coming to tea? This is an excellent choice to delight your company. And it doesn't take long to produce.

PREPARATION TIME 15 MINUTES   SERVES 6
MICROWAVE TIME 7 MINUTES
STANDING TIME 10 MINUTES

- $1/3$ cup all-purpose, unbleached flour
- $1/3$ cup brown sugar
- $1/4$ cup 3-minute rolled oats
- 2   tablespoons honey wheat germ
- 1   teaspoon Oriental five-spice powder or cinnamon
- 3   tablespoons cold unsalted butter, cut up
- $1/4$ cup walnuts

Combine above ingredients in a food processor and pulse on and off until mixture is crumbly, as in making a piecrust. Set aside.

- 2   large or 3 small Golden Delicious apples
- 1   teaspoon lemon juice

Pare, core, and thinly slice apples. Sprinkle with lemon juice and place in an 8-inch microwaveable baking dish lightly sprayed with oil. Cover apples with topping mixture and press down lightly with fingers. Microwave on High for 7 minutes. Let stand 10 minutes before serving. Top with whipped topping, vanilla yogurt, or frozen yogurt if desired.

APRICOT YOGURT PIE

This has to be one of the easiest pies around. Barely a few minutes of your time (plus several hours of chilling in the refrigerator) produce an elegantly smooth, refreshing dessert.

PREPARATION TIME 15 MINUTES   MAKES ONE 9-INCH PIE
CHILLING TIME 3 HOURS OR LONGER

- 12 ounces softened low-fat cream cheese
- 1 cup plain low-fat yogurt
- 3 tablespoons honey
- 1 teaspoon vanilla extract

Beat all ingredients together until smooth.

- 1 baked 9-inch piecrust (see Piecrust with Pecans on page 224)
- ¹/₂ cup canned apricots, drained and chopped

Pour half the cheese-yogurt mixture into the crust, spreading it over the bottom. Spoon apricots evenly over this filling and cover them with the rest of the mixture. Chill for at least 3 hours, or overnight; 30 minutes in the freezer will speed the setting time.

- ³/₄ cup chopped walnuts or pecans

Sprinkle nuts over top of pie before cutting into wedges to serve.

Variation: Other fruits—fresh, frozen, or canned—may be used. Just be sure they're well drained before adding them to the pie.

BAKED APPLES ALLEGRO

Nothing for dessert? If you can round up some firm, crisp, tart-sweet apples, you can have one ready in 15 minutes. If you're not calorie counting, or if dinner was light, add whipped cream or a scoop of ice cream.

PREPARATION TIME 5 MINUTES   SERVES 4
BAKING TIME 10 MINUTES
Preheat oven to 400°.

4 or 5 medium-sized apples
1   tablespoon melted unsalted butter
    Brown sugar, as needed (adjust to tartness of apples)
1   teaspoon brandy
1/4 teaspoon cinnamon

Peel apples, cut them into quarters, and remove the cores. Arrange them in a single layer, core side down, in a baking dish lightly sprayed with oil. Brush apples with melted butter; then sprinkle with sugar, brandy, and cinnamon. Bake in oven for 10 minutes, or until apples are tender. Remove from oven, turn apples over in sauce that has collected in the bottom of the pan, and serve warm.

BANANA AND YOGURT THICK SHAKE

This uses frozen bananas made as described in Bananas Praline (see page 216). Here, however, the bananas are used straight, not rolled in praline.

PREPARATION TIME 3 MINUTES   SERVES 2

28 frozen banana slices (2 bananas)
1   cup nonfat yogurt
1/2 cup skim or low-fat milk
1   tablespoon strawberry jam

Place these ingredients in a blender, put top on, and whip on high speed for 1 minute or more. The shake rises in the blender glass as air is whipped in. Within limits, the longer it's whipped, the thicker it gets. If too thick to drink, add a little skim milk.

Note: An average banana has 12 to 14 slices (1/4 inch thick), and the slices take about 4 hours to freeze.

BANANAS PRALINE

One of the simplest desserts, and one of the most surprisingly delicious, consists of frozen banana chunks. The bananas may be served after dinner as a confection for nibbling.

We like to cut the peeled bananas Oriental style (1-inch diagonal slices), dip and roll the pieces in crushed praline, and then freeze them in a single layer on a baking sheet lined with waxed paper or plastic wrap until solid. After the chunks are frozen, they can be removed from the sheet, dropped into plastic freezer bags, sealed, and returned to the freezer until needed. Don't let them stand long after removing them from the freezer for serving. If they thaw too much, they quickly lose their charm.

Here's an easy way to make the praline for crushing.

PREPARATION TIME 5 MINUTES
FREEZING TIME 4 HOURS

> $1/4$ cup cashew butter or peanut butter
> $1/4$ cup unsalted creamery butter
> 1   cup brown sugar, firmly packed

In a small saucepan, combine the nut butter, creamery butter, and sugar. Place over low heat and stir until sugar melts, about 3 minutes.

> 2   cups crisp rice cereal, coarsely crushed
> 1   cup chopped cashew nuts

Remove pan from heat and stir in rice cereal and nuts. Spread on an oil-sprayed shallow-rimmed pan and allow to cool; then break into pieces and store in airtight containers. To use for Bananas Praline, crush as much as you need in a blender or food processor.

Variations: The bananas can be cut crossways in $1/2$-inch slices and frozen without any coating. These slices can also be rolled in ground nuts or a combination of ground nuts and grated chocolate. They make a good after-school snack. While you are in the freezing mode, you may wish to freeze seedless grapes. They, too, are a wonderful after-school snack.

BANANA STRAWBERRY PIE

Delicious on a hot summer's day.

PREPARATION TIME 15 MINUTES
BAKING TIME 15 MINUTES
CHILLING TIME 45 MINUTES TO 1 HOUR
Preheat oven to 350°.

1	pound tofu
1	large banana
¼	cup honey
3	tablespoons canola oil
2	tablespoons strawberry preserves
1	teaspoon vanilla extract

Blend the above ingredients in a food processor or blender until smooth.

4   fresh strawberries

Add strawberries and mix only long enough to cut the strawberries in small pieces.

1   prepared graham cracker crust

Pour the banana-strawberry mixture into prepared crust and bake for 15 minutes. Allow pie to cool on rack before refrigerating. Place in the freezer 20 minutes before serving.

Note: To make your own graham cracker crust, just place 10 almonds or cashews and 16 squares of graham crackers in a food processor and blend until pulverized. Add 3 tablespoons unsalted butter and process a few more seconds. Press crumb mixture into a 9-inch pie pan and refrigerate while making your filling.

CANTALOUPE CUP

This recipe can be varied in many ways, depending on the fruit at hand. It's equally delightful for breakfast, lunch, or dinner.

PREPARATION TIME 10 MINUTES   **SERVES 2**

- ¹/₄ large, ripe cantaloupe
- 1 seedless orange

Peel and cut cantaloupe into ¹/₄-inch (approximately) cubes. Do the same for the orange.

- 6 seedless red grapes
- 6 seedless green grapes

Cut grapes into halves or thirds, depending on size. You can use grapes that have seeds, but deseeding takes time. You might also use strawberries, blueberries, peaches, nectarines, or kiwis. The latter can be arranged as topping in various decorative ways, in thin slices, halves, or quarters (easiest for eating).

In winter, orange and grapefruit make a good combination. Peel the grapefruit as well as the orange and cut into manageable chunks. You may wish to sweeten overly tart fruit.

CHERRY-BANANA-TOFU PARFAIT

This smooth, creamy, rich-tasting dessert has a high-calorie aura. It is, however, virtually fat-free, and is highly nutritious as well. The best tofu to use is the Japanese silken style that keeps fresh without irradiation, preservatives, or refrigeration. Endless other fruit combinations are possible, so don't worry if you can't find fresh cherries. We offer this version just to get you started.

PREPARATION TIME 15 MINUTES   **SERVES 4**
CHILLING TIME 2 HOURS

- 1 package (10.5 ounces) firm, aseptic-pack silken tofu
- 1 large banana
- 2 tablespoons nonfat plain yogurt
- 1 tablespoon cherry preserves (we use the kind sweetened with fruit-juice concentrate)
- 2 tablespoons dried cherries

3   tablespoons fruit liqueur, such as kirsch, or equal amount of
     fruit juice
1   tablespoon lemon juice
1   teaspoon vanilla
¹/₄ teaspoon salt

Soak the dried cherries in the fruit liqueur or juice until softened. Place them and all other ingredients in a food processor or blender. (If you use a blender, you will have to do this in several batches.) Process until mixture is smooth and creamy, scraping down the sides of container as necessary.

12 to 15 fresh sweet cherries, seeded, and halved or chopped

Fold the cherries by hand into the parfait and spoon it into 4 attractive dessert or wine glasses. Top each with a stemmed cherry. Chill for several hours.

Note: This parfait may be used as a pie filling, then frozen. Allow it to thaw briefly before serving.

CREAMY APRICOT MOUSSE

This delicious concoction can be served alone or, if it is too rich for you, in a smaller portion as a topping over fresh fruit.

PREPARATION TIME 20 MINUTES   **SERVES 4 TO 6**

¹/₂ cup dried apricots (packed loosely)
¹/₂ cup orange juice

Put orange juice and apricots in a medium-sized saucepan and heat to a boil. Turn off heat, cover, and let stand at least 15 minutes.

2   ounces low-fat cream cheese
¹/₂ cup plain low-fat yogurt

Meanwhile, blend cream cheese and yogurt in a processor or blender. Add the apricots and juice and blend until creamy. Store in refrigerator.

¹/₂ cup whipping cream
1   teaspoon vanilla extract

Whip cream and vanilla together until they form whipped cream. Fold the whipped cream gently into the apricot mixture and chill until ready to serve.

FRUIT MÉLANGE WITH CURAÇAO

There are times when a light fruit dessert is the perfect finale to a memorable meal. This mélange is one we have relied on for many years to strike a gentle final chord.

PREPARATION TIME 5 MINUTES   SERVES 6
CHILLING TIME 1 HOUR OR MORE

    6   cups fresh fruit of your choice, such as strawberries, mangoes, bananas, peaches, nectarines, blueberries, grapes
    6   tablespoons frozen orange juice concentrate, partially thawed
    1/4   cup Curaçao liqueur

Peel and pit larger fruit and slice into bite-sized pieces. Place the fruit in a large serving bowl (a glass one is particularly attractive). Combine the undiluted orange juice concentrate with the liqueur and mix with the fruit. Chill fruit mixture thoroughly before serving.

GARDEN OF EDEN MELON

Cantaloupe, honeydew, Crenshaw, and other melons can begin a meal or provide a refreshing ending. Here, a tangy sauce enhances the sweet, subtle flavor of a honeydew.

PREPARATION TIME 5 MINUTES   SERVES 6 TO 8
CHILLING TIME 30 MINUTES

    1   honeydew, cut in wedges
    2   cups sliced or diced peaches
    1   cup sliced strawberries
    1   cup blueberries or raspberries

Be sure melon and other fruits are prime ripe and well chilled.

    1   cup low-fat sour cream
    1   tablespoon honey
    1/2   teaspoon dry mustard
    2   teaspoons lime juice

Stir sauce ingredients together and chill during dinner. When serving, top each wedge of melon with peaches and berries. Let each diner add the sauce.

GRANOLA ROLL

This dessert is especially easy to prepare if you have commercial peanut butter and granola on hand. It's still easy, and perhaps better, if you make them yourself. In a blender or food processor, peanuts can be transformed into peanut butter quickly. (Home-made peanut butter seldom needs added oil.) As for granola, just mix together 3 cups rolled oats, 1 cup wheat germ, 1 cup sesame seeds, 1/4 cup oil, 3/4 cup honey, 1 teaspoon vanilla extract, and a dash of salt. You then spread this mixture evenly on cookie sheets and bake at 325° until golden brown. Stir once or twice for the edges brown first.

To make Granola Roll:

PREPARATION TIME 5 MINUTES   SERVES 4

   1/2   **cup peanut butter**
   1/2   **cup granola**

Blend these two ingredients.

   1/2   **cup raisins**

Work the raisins into the mixture and form a log that's about 1 inch in diameter. Chill. (This can be speeded up by putting the log in your freezer for 5 to 10 minutes before refrigerating it.) Slice when ready to serve.

NECTARINE, BLUEBERRY, AND ALMOND CAKE

When nectarines and blueberries are in season, we make several of these simple yet elegant cakes. They freeze beautifully, and it's great to taste July in February.

PREPARATION TIME 20 MINUTES   SERVES 6
BAKING TIME 30 MINUTES
Preheat oven to 375°.

6	tablespoons unsalted butter, softened
1/3	cup sugar
2	tablespoons brown sugar
1	large egg
2	tablespoons Amaretto liqueur (or 1 tablespoon orange juice, 1/2 teaspoon vanilla, and 1/2 teaspoon almond extract)
1	cup unbleached all-purpose flour
2	teaspoons baking powder
1	pinch salt (optional)
1/3	cup finely ground almonds

Cream butter and sugars together until fluffy. Add egg and Amaretto and beat well. Stir in flour, baking powder, and salt just until well mixed. Stir in ground almonds. Spoon batter evenly into a 9-inch springform pan lightly sprayed with oil.

2	nectarines, sliced
1	cup blueberries, washed and sorted
1/2	teaspoon cinnamon
2	tablespoons sugar (or more if berries are very tart)

Arrange fruit attractively on the batter and press in lightly. Sprinkle with the cinnamon and sugar. Bake in lower third of oven for 20 to 30 minutes, or until cake is nicely browned. Allow cake to cool completely on a rack. Then, before removing the pan's rim, use a sharp knife to loosen any fruit that may have become glued to the edge during baking.

Note: This recipe works with many other fruits. For a slightly more elegant presentation, if you have a little extra time, you may use a lightly oil-sprayed 9-inch tart pan with a fluted rim and removable bottom. With a spoon, spread the batter in the pan as evenly as you can. Chill pan and batter in the freezer for about 15 minutes and then, with your fingers, quickly press the cold mixture around the edges and on the bottom. Add fruit and bake as before, removing outer rim after cake has cooled for 15 minutes. Cool completely before serving.

PEARS, STUFFED AND POACHED   MICROWAVE

No sugar, no water. The pears poach in their own juice. And it's so easy.

PREPARATION TIME 6 MINUTES   SERVES 3
POACHING TIME 6 MINUTES

    3   Bosc pears
    6   dried apricot halves
    6   cloves
    2   tablespoons lemon juice

Peel and core the pears but don't remove stems. Stuff each cavity with two dried
apricot halves, each wrapped around a clove. Brush each pear with lemon juice.
Lay pears in a 1½-quart glass or ceramic casserole and cover. Microwave for 6
minutes on High power (700-watt oven). Serve hot, cool, or cold with mint leaves
and orange slices or mandarin orange segments.

PIECRUST WITH PECANS

Pecans give this tender, crisp piecrust an usually fine flavor. There's no cholesterol present, and the crust is made right in the pie pan—no rolling.

PREPARATION TIME 5 MINUTES   MAKES 1 CRUST
BAKING TIME 15 TO 18 MINUTES
Preheat oven to 400°.

    1¹/₂ cups unbleached, all-purpose flour
    1   teaspoon salt
    1¹/₂ teaspoons sugar

Sift ingredients directly into a 9-inch pie pan.

    ¹/₂   cup finely chopped or ground pecans

Stir pecans into flour mixture with a fork until well blended.

    6   tablespoons canola oil
    3   tablespoons water

Mix oil and water together and pour gradually into the dry ingredients, stirring with a fork until well mixed. If dough is too soft to handle, chill a few minutes in the freezer. With your fingers, press pastry into the bottom and around the sides of the pan, making it as thin and even as possible. Bake immediately or refrigerate for later use.

To bake, prick bottom and sides of the pastry well with a fork, place a sheet of foil over it, and lightly mold it to the shape of the crust. Fill the foil with dried beans and bake for 5 minutes. Reduce heat to 375° and continue baking for 10 to 15 minutes longer. Cool and fill as desired.

TRIPLE-FRUIT CRISP

This dessert combines strawberries for color, bananas for flavorful smoothness, and rhubarb for tart zip. The bananas and strawberries also reduce the need for other sugars.

PREPARATION TIME 20 MINUTES
BAKING TIME 25 MINUTES
Preheat oven to 400°.

SERVES 4

1	pound rhubarb, cut into $1/2$-inch pieces
2	cups strawberries, sliced
2	bananas, sliced
$1/2$	cup strawberry jam
$1^1/2$	tablespoons cornstarch
1	teaspoon grated orange rind
1	teaspoon cinnamon
$1/2$	teaspoon ground cloves
$1/3$ to $1/2$	cup white sugar

If rhubarb stalks are thick, split down middle before cutting into pieces. Combine ingredients and put into 8-by-8-inch baking dish lightly sprayed with oil.

$3/4$	cup rolled oats
$1/2$	cup unbleached, all-purpose flour
2	tablespoons brown sugar
$1/4$	cup walnuts
$1/4$	cup wheat germ
5	tablespoons cold unsalted butter

Blend all ingredients except butter in food processor for 10 or 15 seconds; then cut butter into small pieces and add along with walnuts. Process until mixture appears crumbly. Spread by hand atop fruit mixture. Bake for 25 to 30 minutes. Top should be crisp and bubbly. Serve warm, at room temperature, or cold. Nonfat vanilla topping or frozen low-fat yogurt are options.

Entertaining the Easy Way

According to one authority on entertaining, the most important duty of the successful host is to "create the illusion that you are having as good a time as everyone else." Well, we'd like to say right here that illusions aren't enough for us. If we can't have the real thing, we'd do better to forgo entertaining altogether. In fact, we've heard several accomplished hosts, practitioners of the old-style elegant dinner party, say that they're tired of the whole business and are going to give it up. Dinner parties are just too much work! They will, they say, devise other ways of seeing their friends.

In our minds, though, food and friendship are synergistic, and we'd really hate to give up the tribal ritual of preparing a special meal for our friends on our own turf. So we've taken to using certain tricks, techniques, and corner cutters to minimize the work. We'd like to say we've eliminated the work, but we still have a hang-up about honesty.

Our most popular ploy is a variation of the old-fashioned church basement bit of nostalgia called a *potluck* or *covered-dish* supper, to which everyone contributes a dish to be shared by all. As we recall from our dim Midwestern memories, there was a staggering abundance of good food at those dinners, but usually a hodge-podge of dishes that didn't really go well together. That shortcoming mattered less to us then than it would now.

Usually, our practice is to supply the main dish and then to consult with our friends about what "go with" they would like to bring. We can remember one wonderfully delightful occasion, though, when the guests brought all the food and we merely supplied the setting—put out the company towels, checked the goblets for fingerprints, and turned on the ambience. It was a splendid feast, and we felt like the ultimate liberated host. We knew we had found a better way.

The advantages of cooperative cooking are obvious: No one person has to do all the work. Each contributor can bring a specialty, a dish he or she really enjoys making and does superlatively well. The slight edge of competition that's bound to occur spurs each to greater heights, and the result is a Lucullan banquet that bears little resemblance to the steamy, fragrant, church suppers of our youth.

Another of our favorite approaches to entertaining is an idea we borrowed from restaurants we've visited across the country: the Salad Bar. All the elements of several types of salad are arranged on trays or in bowls, and each guest can choose favorites and come away with a personal expression of what a good salad should be. These events can become humorous, with each person vying to achieve the ultimate salad. With plenty of substantial selections, such as many varieties of marinated beans, prepared grains, pastas, and cheeses included in the display, it's not at all difficult to construct a completely satisfying and delicious meal. The offerings can be as numerous and as elaborate as you wish. And because all the choices are cold, the whole feast can be prepared ahead of time and refrigerated.

Sometimes we make it a Soup and Salad Bar, including several hearty soups (all prepared well ahead and reheated) served in attractive tureens.

Another variation is the Sandwich Buffet. Several kinds of crusty breads and rolls and a collection of possible fillings allow each guest to unleash creative urges and put together something totally mind-boggling. Add a group of garnishes and perhaps a platter of sprouts, and everyone becomes a creative genius. Pocket bread (pita) is particularly good for this type of luncheon because it holds the filling neatly, a definite advantage.

Alternately, you might create a Soup and Sandwich Party, or a Sandwich and Salad Luncheon.

This leads us to the surprising and pleasing meal that consists of nothing but Appetizers. Not a new idea—the Greeks have long had their *mézé*, the Italians their antipasto, the Danes their *smorrebrod*, the Russians their *zakuski*. It's fun occasionally just to nibble our way through the evening. If attention is paid to the variety, quantity, and quality of appetizers presented, it's a stimulating change from the expected and routine way of dining.

Another artful dodge is the Picnic Party. We rely on this one when we haven't the time or inclination to get the house in shelter magazine order. The party can be held on the beach, on a boat (if you—or they—happen to own one), or in some untrafficked park or woodland spot. On occasion, we schedule this picnic to precede a concert or theater performance, when it becomes a Picnic for Patrons of the Arts. We bring the food but never decline if our guests offer to help. We try to make the picnic menu a showstopper, food that is more elegant than common picnic fare but that transports well. A bottle of good wine or champagne, well chilled, doesn't hurt either.

Then there's the Dessert Party, when friends are invited to come after dinner for dessert. We try to have one, two, or sometimes three really special desserts. We usually give this one after we've squirreled away several desserts in the freezer over a period of time, so there's nothing to do but bring them out when the time comes.

There are occasions, of course, when nothing will do but a dinner party of elegance and substance. We seldom, if ever, have the formal sit-down variety. We think we'd need plenty of hired help to pull off such a show; and although time may be more precious than money, sometimes they're both in short supply. We do often have a Sit-down Buffet, at which the guests help themselves and then find a prearranged seat at a preset table.

Because we don't believe in the overwork ethic, we've set up certain methods of operation designed to keep us out of the rest home and allow us to have as much fun as everyone else.

1. Choose dishes that can be completely cooked in advance and frozen or that can be prepared ahead, refrigerated, and then reheated. Try to include some cold dishes.

2. Select dishes that don't deteriorate if they can't be served immediately.

3. Have at least one very special, impressively attractive dish—it can be a main course or a dessert—because how food looks is just as important as how it tastes and it's certainly true that we often "eat with our eyes." Pay special attention to handsome serving utensils and garnishes; they can make all the difference. If you're inexperienced at garnishing, make a habit of collecting attractive food photos from magazines to inspire you.

4. After deciding on the menu, assemble the recipes and write out a shopping list. Plan your shopping time to coincide as closely as possible to preparation time so that fruits, vegetables, and other foods will be at their peak when you use them.

5. Prepare as much of the food in advance as possible. Try to leave only the salad and reheating of other dishes for the day of the party. If you plan to have a molded or marinated salad, even that can be done the day before.

6. Don't attempt major cleaning at the last minute. Do a thorough job several days before; then give the house minor touch-ups each day to keep things in order.

7. Set the table and arrange the decorations the night before, if possible. Make a collection of interesting and dramatic objects to use in imaginative ways for centerpieces or coverings on a buffet table. They need not be rare or expensive. (Junk shops often yield great treasures at low cost.) Use what is at hand. For example, a blanket of fresh green fern fronds can make an exotic, disposable table covering for a summer buffet. Try to get away from the old candles-and-flowers routine. Spend some time, when time is cheap, arranging your decorative objects in interesting ways, and you'll hardly have to think about how to do it when party time arrives.

8. If you're serving drinks, have them premixed and ready for the ice. Have limes and oranges sliced, lemon peel pared, coasters at the ready. Wine is easier to serve than mixed drinks, so don't discourage this preference. Be sure to have non-alcoholic beverages for those who request them. If you can, chill glasses.

9. If you have a *compañero* (spouse, roommate, significant other, et cetera), work out a shared system of serving and clearing away, with a clear definition of who's to do what and when.

10. If the party is large, minimize the after-party cleanup by using disposable goblets, dishes, napkins, and tablecloths. There are attractive ones available.

Arrange for their neat, unobtrusive disposal between courses and at the end of the meal. One way is to have a helper circulate with a large plastic bag.

11. Small children love parties and when allowed to participate often display great poise and decorum until the stimulation of the party atmosphere affects their young adrenals. Delinquency then ensues. Here are some preventive measures: (a) Have them fed and tucked away before the party begins (often difficult to accomplish and keep accomplished). (b) Have a competent baby-sitter look after them during the party. A TV or movie tape can keep them occupied, and the sitter can trot them out for a brief, charming appearance. (c) Deposit them at the home of a playmate for the night. You can probably make a reciprocal deal.

12. Older children can be something else. Depending on their age and motivation, they can help, enjoy it, and gain experience. They can park cars, answer the door and telephone, take wraps, help prepare and serve food, and even clean up afterward.

13. Pets tend to be effusive in their display of friendliness, so they should be kept restrained. They might scratch that new Honda Prelude.

14. Post a menu where you can check it at serving time. That way, you won't find something in the refrigerator the next day that you forgot to serve.

15. Unless you live in the Mojave, have an alternative spot ready if your party is to be alfresco. Whenever our garden is very dry, we plan to serve outdoors. There is nothing like it to break the drought.

You may be wondering if we entertain only vegetarians. In our present circle of friends, the vegetarians are greatly outnumbered. But we never feel we must add meat to the menu to keep them happy. We've discovered that the nonvegetarians find the experience of vegetarian dishes novel, interesting, satisfying—and delicious. They often seem surprised and delighted that they've gotten through a whole meal with no trace of meat and haven't really missed it. And besides, they haven't come just for the food. They've come to spend time with us in our home because they are our friends.

Helpful Hints

(To improve a dish and/or speed its preparation)

*Pour various dry measurements into your hand. When you do, memorize how each measurement looks. Eventually, you should be able to get along occasionally without measuring spoons.

*To peel an onion more easily, cut off ends, cut it in half, and peel each half. Better yet, cut it in quarters.

*Potatoes will bake faster if put in very hot water for 10 minutes and then dried before baking.

*If you've put too much salt in something you're cooking, add raw potato slices. They'll absorb the salt. When the dish is done, discard them.

*When you double a recipe, don't double the salt. Instead, use half again as much; then taste to see if it needs more.

*One of the best ways to decorate a dish of food is with an edible flower, such as a daylily, marigold, or violet.

*Use an ice-cream scoop for putting batter in muffin tins. A scoop holds just the right amount. It's also handy in forming patties. Then pat down the mound.

*A bit of sugar coaxes out the flavor of a tomato.

*Often, the red tomatoes you buy are red in color only. Treat them as if they're green and keep them for a week; you'll usually find them much improved.

*Use yogurt instead of oil or cream as a thickener. For salad dressing: add 1 tablespoon oil and 3 tablespoons yogurt to 1/4 teaspoon Dijon mustard, salt, pepper, and 2 tablespoons wine vinegar.

*Don't wash domestic rice. It doesn't need washing and you lose nutrients. To wash foreign and talc-coated rice, put it in a saucepan and tilt the pan while you run water slowly over it. Keep the water flowing until it runs clear.

*The best way to handle leaf lettuce is to wash its leaves and spin them dry as soon as you get home from market. Place in a plastic bag with crumpled paper towels in the bottom. Then store the closed bags in your refrigerator's vegetable drawer. The lettuce is then always ready for use. The paper towels absorb excess water that makes lettuce rot.

*Brown rice soaked overnight cooks in about the same time as white rice.

*Barley usually takes 45 to 50 minutes to cook. Soak it for 5 hours or overnight, and it will cook in 15 minutes.

*Put the stems of things like parsley, dill, coriander, and watercress in a glass of water and cover top loosely with a plastic bag. Then store in the refrigerator. They'll keep much longer. Asparagus keeps better that way, too. Trim off stem ends first. Be sure no leaves are under water.

*The best way to quickly renew the cutting edge of a knife is to stroke it a few times on a steel. You've seen butchers do it.

*Peel fresh ginger, immerse in a jar of vodka, and refrigerate; it will keep indefinitely. Vodka imparts no taste and is an excellent preservative.

*Always use cold tap water for cooking, never hot. Hot water absorbs lead, copper, cadmium, and other undesirable elements from piping. For the same reason, let cold water run first thing in the morning until it runs fresh and cold. That helps get rid of the elements it picked up standing overnight.

*Firm or regular tofu will work for almost any recipe. Extra firm is good for kabobs.

*When baking sweet potatoes, put foil on rack below. It will keep drippings from going to the bottom of the oven.

*If flour is cold, warm it before using for baking. Cold flour retards yeast action.

*If you want to prepare a casserole ahead of time, bake it for all but 20 minutes of its baking time. Cool; then cover and keep in the refrigerator until 30 minutes before it's to be served. Then put it in a preheated oven. In 10 minutes, the chilled casserole will be warm. The next 20 minutes will complete the baking.

*Slice a loaf of bread before freezing it. That way, you can take what you need without thawing out the whole loaf.

*Cheese tastes best at room temperature. Remove from the refrigerator 30 to 60 minutes before use to allow it to warm. Exceptions: Cottage cheese and cream cheese are best when removed from the refrigerator just before serving.

*To peel garlic more easily, put cloves in a dishtowel and whack them with the flat side of a cleaver or wide, heavy knife. A cutting board with a handle is also a good whacking tool.

*A little salt will bring out the flavor of chocolate.

*Before measuring honey, spread a film of oil on the measuring spoon or cup. The honey will slide off easily and leave no residue.

*Head lettuce stays greener longer if its core has been removed. Remove core by striking its end against a hard surface. The core can then be pulled or twisted out.

*Though red lentils are harder to find than brown, they cook much faster than brown, in about 10 minutes instead of 40. You can use the red variety in any recipe calling for lentils.

*To make wooden handles ovenproof, wrap them in a double thickness of aluminum foil.

*Before grating cheese, brush a little oil on the grater with a pastry brush. This will make cleaning the grater easier.

*To convert cottage cheese into a low-calorie "cream cheese," put the cottage cheese in a food processor and process with steel knife until smooth. (A dry cottage cheese works better than creamed cottage cheese.)

*A big time-saver is arranging spices in alphabetical order in a rack. Arrange canned goods by type whenever possible.

*You can whip canned evaporated milk if it is very cold. The bowl in which you whip it and the beater should also be very cold.

*Corn silk is best removed from an ear of corn by rubbing with a wadded paper towel.

*Don't automatically throw out food amounts that are "too small to save." They're often just what you need to thicken a soup.

Index